THE TEEN'S GUIDE
TO PERSONAL FINANCE

THE TEEN'S GUIDE TO PERSONAL FINANCE

Basic concepts in personal finance that every teen should know

Joshua Holmberg and David Bruzzese

Foreword by BJ Fuller, Ph.D.

iUniverse, Inc.
New York Bloomington Shanghai

The Teen's Guide to Personal Finance
Basic concepts in personal finance that every teen should know

iUniverse books may be ordered through booksellers or by contacting:

iUniverse
1663 Liberty Drive
Bloomington, IN 47403
www.iuniverse.com
1-800-Authors (1-800-288-4677)

Because of the dynamic nature of the Internet, any Web addresses or links contained in this book may have changed since publication and may no longer be valid.

The information, ideas, and suggestions in this book are not intended to render professional advice. Before following any suggestions contained in this book, you should consult your personal accountant or other financial advisor. Neither the author nor the publisher shall be liable or responsible for any loss or damage allegedly arising as a consequence of your use or application of any information or suggestions in this book.

ISBN: 978-0-595-50969-0 (pbk)
ISBN: 978-0-595-61714-2 (ebk)

Printed in the United States of America

Contents

Foreword

BJ Fuller, Ph. D.
Co-Founder, BJ Buzz
Organization and Management Consulting
Former Human Resources Vice President, Compaq Computer

Success in most areas of life depends on having the right tools, knowing how to use them and developing the discipline to use those tools as a matter of habit. This is especially true of financial tools and spending habits. In my practice I find that the positive habits of self-discipline, in any aspect of life, carry through from adolescence and have a major influence on our success, whether it's in working with others, in raising our families, or in managing our finances.

This is a time in our culture when teenagers are tempted every day to make poor financial choices—using credit cards, failing to pay off debts, spending rather than saving—and these choices have long-term consequences. Many young adults end up with little savings, have to borrow even more to pay higher education expenses, and are saddled with high interest debt for years into their adulthood. This often leads to a long struggle of trying to pay down credit card debt, student loans, and second mortgages.

Knowing and using effective financial tools and techniques is the key to avoiding these struggles. It's difficult for young people to find resources to help them understand financial tools and to learn how to apply them in daily decision making. Their parents often grew up in a very different financial world: one without easy credit, skyrocketing tuition expenses, and without the savings tools that are available today such as the 401(k).

This book provides a clear and accessible roadmap for understanding today's financial realities, the tools that are available, and when and how they should be used. The book also addresses the mindset that young people must develop in order to make using these tools a part of their everyday financial decisions. Following these guidelines can help lead to the development of positive money management habits based on a solid understanding of the basic concepts that shape today's financial world.

I recommend that both parents and teenagers read this book and discuss how they can work together to build a strong financial foundation for the young person's future. Waiting is not an option. Many of the recommendations in this book yield far greater benefit if implemented early in life—in the teenage and young adult years. The book includes easy-to-follow action plans that will make an immediate difference in the financial wellbeing of the young people who follow this guidance.

Preface

It's no surprise that a record number of Americans are declaring bankruptcy while consumer debt and home foreclosures are at an all time high. Many adults simply don't have the basic financial knowledge to safely navigate today's environment of predatory lending, identity theft, and nonstop consumer marketing. What's more, they don't know how to use the valuable financial tools they do have. We've all read stories of good, hard-working and well intended people suddenly finding themselves in serious financial problems that put them at risk of losing the very homes and savings they have worked so hard to obtain for their families—we want to help you not get caught in such a situation. The good news is that it's not that hard and we know you can do it.... . but you must learn these concepts and act now. We'll show you how.

Unprepared for the financial responsibilities imposed on us when we entered the working world for the first time, we saw our earnings as a way to improve our lives in the short term. With money, we could acquire some of the things we wanted, but really didn't need. With the numbers of advertisements that daily bombard Americans—and particularly teenagers and young adults—it is no surprise that those wants are great; greater, in fact, than concerns about future financial stability and the rewards that come with it.

As authors, we are challenged to share with you the importance of making the right decisions *now,* because doing so will significantly affect your likelihood of achieving financial independence in the future. And with financial independence, you will be in better control of your life. We certainly could have benefited from this information in our teenage years.

As childhood friends, we grew up like most kids without giving much thought to financial goals, saving or investing. Neither of us was taught the simple financial concepts that could have helped us avoid hard-learned financial lessons while getting an early start on becoming financially independent.

Like many of you, we had parents who did their best to try to help us learn about concepts of personal money management. Many parents understand the need to educate their kids about finances and do their best to help them, but because they were never taught some of the key concepts themselves, their ability to help their kids is limited. In other cases, kids simply aren't ready to hear their parents' suggestions. Whatever your personal situation, we're confident that the concepts here will be useful tools for parents and kids alike in helping to talk about planning for your future while enjoying your life today.

Having learned these concepts on our own, well after our teenage years, it is our goal to educate and better prepare you to make informed decisions that will give you a head start on the road to a secure and independent financial future. We also think this will help you have useful conversations with parents, grandparents, other relatives or friends about how to help you with your plan.

Acknowledgements

Thanks to our wives, Nicole Holmberg and Ann Bruzzese

Thanks to our editor, Joie Norby

Also, thanks to all of those who contributed, including Ray Kagiyama, Shelley & Andy Sheridan, and Brad Cochennet

Introduction

The Teen's Guide to Personal Finance is for young adults who are taking the first steps toward financial independence. This journey can be complex and challenging, but the decisions made along the way—and especially early in life—can have profound effects on one's ultimate financial wellbeing. In fact, more and more Americans fail to achieve financial independence because of decisions they make in their teens, 20s and 30s. Many become financially indebted to others and are unable to take total control of their lives. Some of the decisions leading to these circumstances are undoubtedly made on purpose, but others are made because of a lack of basic financial knowledge and information. Our goal is to teach you some basic concepts that will help you to avoid financial pitfalls and make informed decisions that will have a significant impact on your life. The sooner you understand these concepts, the better equipped you will be. After all, you have on your side one of the most valuable of all financial assets: time.

But time can also be one of your worst enemies. The financial responsibilities and realities that come with adulthood may now seem far away. However, take a moment to think about the following: How many of your peers know what they will be doing in a year? After college? At retirement age? What about you? We know what it's like to live in the moment, not wanting to be bothered by an uncertain future. After all, we were teenagers, too. Work, investing, and retirement weren't exactly things we spent a long time thinking about when we were in high school. Like us, most teenagers give these issues little consideration.

It is important to understand that financial independence is not necessarily wealth. Rather, financial independence is a state of being that allows you to use money to generate wealth, help the less fortunate, or do whatever else you want to do with it. You may not have a large sum of money when you first become financially independent, but you will have at least enough to be in control of your life from a financial perspective. Financial independence means freedom: freedom to do what you want with your money and freedom from the bonds of bad debt, creditors, employers, the government, and others who are more than happy to use your dependence on money to control—or at least significantly influence—your life. Financial independence is not something that only can be achieved late in life. You can achieve financial independence now or in the near future, if you're up to the task. But just as it can be achieved, financial independence can be lost, so once it's in your grasp, you'll need to work to maintain it.

Failing to Plan
Is Planning to Fail

Before you take a single step on your path to financial independence, you should understand where it is you want to go, and then figure out how to get there. Just as you might plan a road trip, you must look at a map in order to choose your best route. On the journey to financial independence, you should also ask yourself if you have the self-discipline to reach your goals, because you will be faced with many difficult choices along the way. Some will make the journey shorter, some longer, and others may make completing the journey nearly impossible. We guarantee that there are no ways to magically reach your destination, but if you make a good plan and stick to it, you *will* get there. We are here to help.

Setting Goals

You may have the goal of going to a particular college or entering a certain field of work when you graduate. These are important milestones, and like other goals, they have financial implications. If you decide you're going to college, how much will it cost and how much of that amount do you expect to pay? Will you borrow money from your family? Will you pay with your savings? Will you take out student loans? Will you work while you're in school? How much can you expect to owe when you graduate? If you're going straight into the workforce, how much do you expect to earn? Where do you want to live? If you plan on living away from your parents, how will you afford rent or a mortgage, utilities, food, and other bills?

These are important short-term decisions you need to make. The farther in advance you can plan for these issues, the better off you will be because you can start saving and making other financial preparations right away. Again, if you know what to expect on your journey, you will be much better off. Identifying major milestones is a good place to start. Some questions you might ask yourself are: Where do you want to be in five years, after you graduate from college, or after you have been working for a while? What about at your ten-year high school reunion? In twenty years? What kind of lifestyle do you want? When do you want to retire? Once you are able to realistically answer any or all of these questions, it is important that you put your goals on paper and review them periodically so that you know if you're on the right track.

Action Plan

Let's get started! Think about your goals and then write them down in the space provided below. Consider the example of Stephan, a 17-year-old high school student. Stephan is a B-level student who works part-time at a fast food restaurant. When we asked Stephan about his goals, he answered as follows:

1. At this time next year, I want to: *have my own car and have saved $3,500 in my college fund.*

2. Three years from now, I want to: *be at the State University studying Journalism.*

3. Five years from now, I want to: *have graduated from college and be earning at least $40,000 per year working full time.*

4. 10 years from now, I want to: *have doubled my starting salary, earning at least $80,000 per year, and own my own home.*

Now you try it. Fill in the blanks below with your own goals:

1. At this time next year, I want to: _____

    _____

2. Three years from now, I want to: _____

    _____

3. Five years from now, I want to: _____

    _____

4. 10 years from now, I want to: _____

    _____

Five years after speaking to us about his goals, Stephan is well on his way to achieving them. He recently graduated from college and got a good job in his chosen field. Although he is still working toward his 10-year goal of doubling his salary, he now has new three, five and 10-year goals that include saving for an early retirement.

If you are financially independent, you will be able to make your own lifestyle choices. If not, someone else will make them for you. It's that simple. Like many Americans who do not achieve or maintain financial independence, you may be faced with the dilemma of wanting to retire but needing to work, or not being able to afford the things you want or even need.

Whatever your goals may be, it is important that you write them down and review them periodically. Just thinking about them isn't enough. If you write them down, you'll be better equipped to track your progress. It's also normal for goals to change, so be prepared to make adjustments along the way.

Now that you have set some goals, let's look at some important concepts that will help you make your goals a reality.

Time Is on Your Side

When I was 12 years old, I got my first job mowing lawns in my neighborhood. Every Saturday, I would get up early and head out for a long morning of cutting grass. Most of my customers paid me in cash or with checks, and because I didn't have a bank account at the time, my father kept the money for me, except for $20, which I kept as spending money. He told me he would pay me 10 cents a month for every dollar that he held for me. He said he was paying me not to spend my money. "You mean if I don't spend my money, you'll give me more?" I asked. "That's right," he said. "And it's not just because you're my son. Other people will pay you, too." After giving it some thought, I figured out this was a much easier way to make money than mowing lawns. Little did I know I had just received my first lesson about earning interest.

Eventually, when I could drive, I got a savings account at a local bank and continued my savings plan. Over the years, I got a few more customers, but I always put away most of the money and kept a small amount for spending. When I went away to college, I got a part time job at a café near campus and continued to put away money from every paycheck, although with college expenses, I was saving less than I was spending. But the habit I had developed with my lawn mowing business made saving automatic, and slowly, my account grew. Most of this growth was due to my regular deposits, but I was also earning interest on the entire balance. In addition, the interest I earned was also earning interest.

After I graduated and got a job as a biologist, I had ten percent of my paycheck automatically deducted and put into my retirement account, which was *invested in mutual funds. I'm now 48 years old and have accumulated more than $1 million. The funny thing is that a lot of that money was given to me by complete strangers who wanted to pay me for not spending my money.*

—*Sean*
Denver, Colorado

Sean's story is quite uncommon. For many people, the habit of saving or investing money is not started early in life, which makes saving or investing later in life much more difficult. Fortunately, Sean's father began teaching him about earning interest at an early age. His father knew about the *time value of money*. The basic concept of the time value of money is that a dollar today is worth more than a dollar in the future. Why? Because of interest. With interest, the dollar you have in your hand can be put to work in an interest-bearing investment like a savings account where it can earn more money for you.

As an example, if you receive $100 today and deposit it in a 5 percent, interest-bearing account, it will have earned $5 in one year and will be worth $105 a year from now. Similarly, if you received $100 a year ago and placed it in a 5 percent, interest-bearing account, it would be worth $105 today. However, if you *did not* place the money in an interest-bearing account, it would still be worth $100 (assuming you didn't spend it) in one year, effectively costing you $5 of value.

Let's look at a couple of additional examples of how interest works for you:

Simple Interest:
Simple interest is calculated only on the beginning value. For example, if you were to receive 5 percent simple interest on a beginning value of $100, you would get 5 percent of $100 in the first year, or $5.

If you continue to receive 5 percent simple interest on the original $100, over several years your investment would grow as follows:

Year 1: 5% of $100 = $5 + $100 = $105
Year 2: 5% of $100 = $5 + $105 = $110
Year 3: 5% of $100 = $5 + $110 = $115
Year 4: 5% of $100 = $5 + $115 = $120
Year 5: 5% of $100 = $5 + $120 = $125

Simple interest gives you an idea of how interest affects the time value of your money, but the financial world depends on an even more powerful form of interest: *compound interest.*

Compound Interest:
Compound interest is calculated not only on the beginning principle, but also on the interest earned during the investment period. Compound interest and simple interest are identical in the first interest cycle, which was one year in our previous example. However, using the example below, years two through five begin to show the power of compound interest.

If you received 5 percent interest compounded yearly on a beginning value of $100, you would get 5 percent of $100 in the first year, or $5. The second year, however, the interest is calculated on the beginning amount of year two, which would be $105, not $100 as in the simple interest example above. Therefore, you will earn more in year two than in year one because you are paid interest *on the interest*—$5—you made in year one. The table below shows compound interest over a period of five years with a $100 initial investment:

Year 1: 5% of $100.00 = $5.00 + $100.00 = $105.00
Year 2: 5% of $105.00 = $5.25 + $105.00 = $110.25
Year 3: 5% of $110.25 = $5.51 + $110.25 = $115.76
Year 4: 5% of $115.76 = $5.79 + $115.76 = $121.55
Year 5: 5% of $121.55 = $6.08 + $121.55 = $127.63

Over many years, the power of compound interest is staggering. The longer the whole amount is invested, the greater the return, not because you keep earning interest on the original dollar, but because you earn *interest on the interest*. Thus, the longer money is allowed to grow, the larger the pool of money becomes and the more interest it can earn (earning 10 percent of $1,000 is much greater than earning 10 percent of $100). The following graph shows how a single $500 investment earning 10 percent interest annually grows to nearly $8,000—or nearly 16 times the original $500 investment—over a period of thirty years (assuming 10 percent annual return and all interest reinvested).

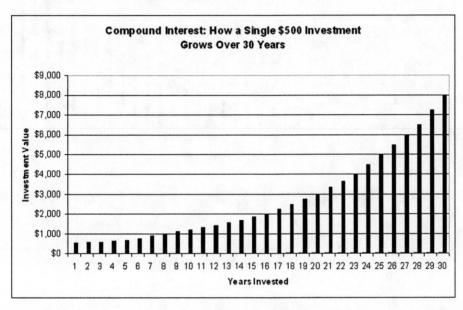

As the graph above illustrates, interest earnings in the early years are fairly small—only $50 in year one for example. However, as the investment begins to earn interest on the entire balance, the interest earnings between year 29 and 30 is $721!

Now let's look at another example of compound interest. If you invested $500 *every year* for thirty years and it grew at the same interest rate as the example above, you would have a whole lot more money—not only because of the annual $500 deposits, but because of the effect of compound interest. In fact, you would earn more than $8,000 in *interest alone* between years twenty-nine and thirty, which is the amount of the final balance in the first scenario. That's not a bad trade off for *not* spending your money.

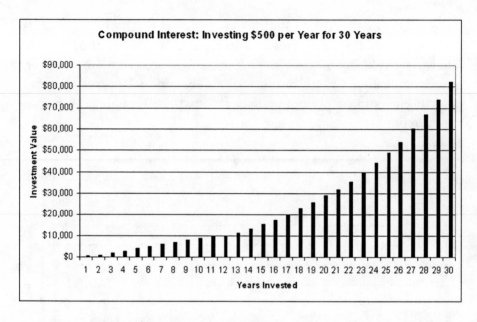

Looking back at your goals, you probably plan to earn a lot more than $5,000 per year when you enter the workforce. At the time of writing, a one-person household with a gross yearly income of less than $9,570 was defined by the federal government as being at the poverty level. If you invest just 10 percent of what you earn every year, your compound interest earnings could be much greater than the $82,000 shown in the chart above.

The reason we say "could be" instead of "will be" is because of two variables: the amount you choose to invest every year and the *rate of return*, or interest rate, earned by your investments. Because interest rates vary, so will your interest earnings. Even a slight change in the rate of return on your investments can have a significant effect on earnings over time, as illustrated in the following chart. You can see that just a two percent difference in the interest rate results in a 42 percent value difference in 30 years.

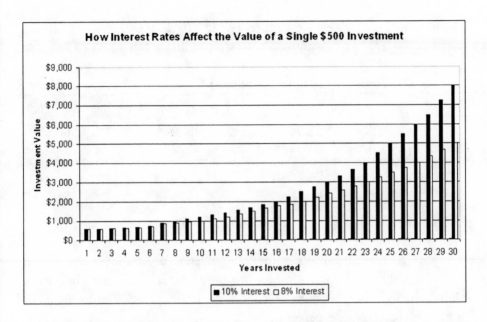

As we mentioned before, interest rates are only part of the equation. The other variable to consider is how much you invest each year. You will have to make this decision based on what you earn, your expenses, and what you are willing to put away. To help you determine how much you should be investing now, take a look back at your goals. If you want to have $20,000 to pay for college, for example, you'll need to consider how many years you have to invest and then how much you need to commit per year to reach your goal.

Using this example, if you have five years to generate $20,000, you would need to invest $4,000 per year, or roughly $333 per month ($20,000 ÷ 5 years = $4000, ÷ 12 months = $333.33). With the help of compound interest, your monthly out-of-pocket investment would drop to $275— less than $10 per day. We know this still seems like a lot, but if you think of investing on a *daily* basis, your goal may not seem so formidable.

The table below shows how much saving $10, $20 and $30 per day can amount to over time, assuming a compound interest rate of 8 percent[1]:

Years	Saving $10/day	Saving $20/day	Saving $30/day
1	$3,735	$7,470	$11,205
5	$22,043	$44,086	$66,129
10	$54,883	$109,767	$164,651
20	$176,706	$353,412	$530,118
35	$688,165	$1,376,329	$2,064,494
50	$2,379,518	$4,759,036	$7,138,554

If your goal is to become a millionaire, invest as much as you can as soon as you can. The table below shows you how long it will take to become a millionaire by saving between $10 per day and $30 per day, assuming compound interest rate of 8 percent:

Savings Per Day	Time to become a millionaire
$10	40 years
$20	32 years
$30	27 years

Considering the value of time, if you start investing when you are eighteen, save just $1,000 a year for eighteen years, and then let the total amount continue to compound based on the 12 percent average annual rate of return for the U.S. stock market, you will have more than $1 million by the time you are sixty-one years old. That's not a bad return on an $18,000 investment! Did you ever imagine that it could be so easy to become a millionaire?

---

1   Assuming a daily savings over a typical month of 30 days

How Can I Start Saving?

Let's cut to the chase: saving is difficult. Many people have told us that they actually feel hopeless and totally frustrated at not being able to save. It's no wonder why. First, considerable amount of our paychecks are taken away from us through tax withholdings and other payroll deductions before we can even touch it (we'll take a look at this in a subsequent chapter). What's more, nearly every waking moment of our lives, we are bombarded by advertisements that try to get us to purchase certain kinds of food, the coolest new clothes, all the best new video games, music, and other things. We work hard for our money, and we want to enjoy it and reward ourselves for our hard work. If saving were easy, there wouldn't be books written on the subject and Americans wouldn't have such extreme levels of debt. That being said, there are some strategies that can be very effective when put to use for your savings plan. We know that you can gain control of this part of your life and begin your journey simply by learning and applying the few simple concepts we will cover next.

Pay yourself first

We remember the first time we heard the saying "pay yourself first." How can you pay yourself first when a big chunk of your money is gone before you even receive your paycheck? That's a good question, and the answer reinforces the point we're trying to make.

When taxes are withheld from your paycheck, you might complain and wish you had more money, but you learn to deal with it. You have no other

11

choice. So you keep your spending in line with the amount of money you have left over, and if you can't afford something, you wait until you receive your next paycheck to buy it.

The same philosophy drives the "pay yourself first" mentality. Think about how much money you can "pay yourself" from each paycheck. Is it 10 percent of your gross earnings? Maybe 5 percent or 15 percent? Pick an amount that you can realistically save and "pay yourself" that amount of money from every single paycheck. Put it in your savings account, send it to your broker, or sock it away in your retirement account, but whatever you do, don't spend it. It might be painful at first not to have this money available for dates or going out with your friends, but just like the money the government takes, you will learn to deal with it. By making "paying yourself first" automatic, you will quickly learn to adjust your lifestyle as needed and after awhile, you probably won't even notice it's gone … it's true!

Once you're comfortable with paying yourself first, you will be amazed at how quickly your savings or investments begin to grow. Also, you will be reinforcing the disciplined spending behavior that will keep you on the right track toward financial independence that so few people in America ever learn.

So chuckle all you want about paying yourself first, and then go do it. When you get a raise, rather than increasing your spending level (as the advertisers are hoping you will), pay yourself *even more* with the extra earnings. Soon you will have a large savings account or investment portfolio for your college education, a down payment on your own house, money for retirement, or whatever else you set as your goal.

Consider the following story about Simon, an 18-year-old high school senior from Tempe, Arizona:

> *I thought I had everything last year when I was a junior. My parents helped me buy a new car, I had a steady girlfriend, and I worked enough at night and on weekends to afford just about everything I wanted. I went out with friends or with my girlfriend several nights a week, and everyone always wanted to ride in my car when we went out for lunch. Also, I had enough money to buy a cool new camera cell phone for $250.*

Over the summer, I started looking into colleges and I recently got accepted to my top choice. Because my parents couldn't afford to pay for my education, I applied for financial aid. Due to my part-time job during high school, the college seemed to think that I should have money available for tuition. Unfortunately, I don't have a dime.

I thought about all the money I had spent over the past couple of years going out on dates, buying gas, going to lunch, and paying for that crazy cell phone, not to mention all the text messaging charges. If I had given more thought to paying myself instead of paying everyone else from my paycheck, I would be in a much better position to pay for college. Now it looks like I'll be going to the local community college, which I can afford, and living at home.

Simon's story is very common among teenagers. We all want the best new clothes, cars and gadgets, but instant gratification may come with a steep price in the future, such as limiting your college funds. Had Simon not used his camera phone so often, his purchase of the phone and associated bills could have beefed up his college savings account by over $600.

Understanding the Difference between Needs and Wants

If you're like other young adults, you probably *want* many things: a new iPod, a certain car, clothes, music, etc. But what do you really *need*? While you are still dependent on your parents, your basic needs are almost certainly being met. There is food in the refrigerator, you have clothes to wear and a place you can call home. Your most basic human needs are satisfied, and the rest of the things you think you need are likely things you *want*. Knowing the difference between needs and wants is important because it will help you make choices about your financial future. Imagine you are on a road trip and have only $5 in your pocket. You *need* to buy $5 worth of gas to reach your final destination, but you also *want* to buy a snack. When you reach the gas station, what will you do?

Budgeting

An important tool for saving money is a budget. A budget provides an understanding of where our money comes from and where it goes. Not only will a budget inform you of where you are spending your money, but it will also allow you to know how much money you have to spend over a certain time period. You've heard of budgets before and possibly thought that they would be hard to do; We'll show you that developing and using budgets is not hard and can actually be kind of fun and rewarding.

The following chart is a basic budget worksheet. You may need to add rows for additional information not included, or leave rows blank for items that don't apply to you. It is important to be as detailed as possible. If you know you took $40 out of the ATM but don't know what you spent it on, include it as "ATM, not categorized" and start keeping track of your cash transactions.

	Month 1	**Month 2**	**Month 3**	**Average** Add months 1-3 and divide by 3
Employment Income, after tax (take home pay)				
Other income				
TOTAL INCOME				
Rent				
Utilities: electricity, gas, water, etc.				
Telephone				
Cable TV				
ATM, not categorized				
Insurance				
Car payment				
Gas				

Groceries				
Eating Out				
Credit card #1				
Credit card #2				
Other debt payment				
TOTAL PAYMENTS				
NET SAVINGS				

Now that you have filled out your budget worksheet, subtract your *total payments* from your *total income* for each month and then average the three. If your net savings is a positive number, good for you! You are making more money than you are spending, which is a fantastic first step toward achieving your financial goals.

If your net savings is a negative number, however, it means that you are spending more money that you are bringing in. The only way you can continue this trend is to exhaust your assets or pile up debt. Closely analyze the payments you entered in the worksheet to determine what you need less of or can completely eliminate.

Continue to analyze your monthly budget and always try to bring in more money than you are spending. It may take some time to figure out where your money is going and to determine where you can reduce your expenditures, but eventually you will understand that some of the things you are paying for are wants rather than needs, and reducing the payments on those things can help your net savings.

Action Plan

Start saving now. Remember: time is your most valuable asset. This is a phrase that should always be on your mind, especially when you're thinking about making a purchase. If you don't start saving now, when are you going to start? When you get a raise? After you go to college? When you get married? The bottom line is that if you don't start now, you might never start, or you'll start so late in life that it will be nearly impossible to ever become financially independent.

If you're still having trouble, think about your spending habits. Your budget is a good tool for you to use for a conversation with your parents, grandparents, teacher or friend to get their ideas and support on how you can make your budget work. With your budget and ideas from others, you'll be able to consider additional sources to find the money to "pay yourself first." Making slight changes to how you spend your money can amount to significant savings over the course of month and a year:

Suggestion	Monthly Savings	Yearly Savings
Save 50 cents per day in loose change	$15	$180
Take your lunch to school (estimated $4/day)	$80	$960
Reduce eating out by 2 times per month	$30	$360
Avoid checking and ATM fees	$7	$84
Substitute tap water for 1 can of soda per day	$15	$180
Shop around for the cheapest gas for your car	$4	$48
Pay bills on time to avoid late fees	$20	$240
Postpone buying until things are on sale	$25	$300
	$196	$2,352

The savings in the chart above can add up over time. Assume that you can save $196 per month by cutting out unnecessary spending. Let's look at what that money can earn over time, assuming a 10 percent return:

After 5 years	After 10 years	After 20 years
$15,178	$40,150	$148,836

As you can see, slightly reducing the amount of money you spend on everyday items such as lunch, soda and gas can significantly add up in the amount you are capable of saving. If you analyze how you are currently spending your money, we are sure you can come up with a dozen more ways to reduce those expenses and pay yourself first from each and every paycheck. You might even think of ways to make this kind of fun by setting goals with your family and challenging yourselves to meet your saving (and not spending) goals, like a game where you all check in on your progress every month.

Understanding Your Paycheck

Before you start saving and can take advantage of compound interest on your money, you need to earn some money. We understand that many teenagers will work jobs that don't provide a typical paycheck. If you baby sit, mow lawns, or buy and sell things on E-Bay for money, you are probably paid with cash or a personal check. If so, this section may not apply to you, but eventually you will receive a conventional paycheck, so refer back to this chapter at the appropriate time to understand the meaning of your paycheck.

If you are employed, you should expect a paycheck similar to the one described below. Most likely, you will be paid based on the number of hours you work. When this book was written, the minimum hourly wage in the U.S. was $5.85 per hour.

As your first payday approaches, you will undoubtedly be excited to receive your earnings. You might assume that working 40 hours at a wage of $8 per hour will provide you with a paycheck of $320. But in most cases, your actual spending power, or take-home pay, will be much less than what you earned.

Many types of deductions can be taken from your *gross earnings*, which is the amount of money you earn before anything is deducted. These paycheck deductions may include federal tax, state tax, local tax, health insurance, life insurance, disability insurance, retirement plan, union dues, and more. What is left of your paycheck after all the deductions is called *net earnings*. The chart below illustrates how gross earnings in a $320 paycheck might be "divided" into tax withholdings and net earnings:

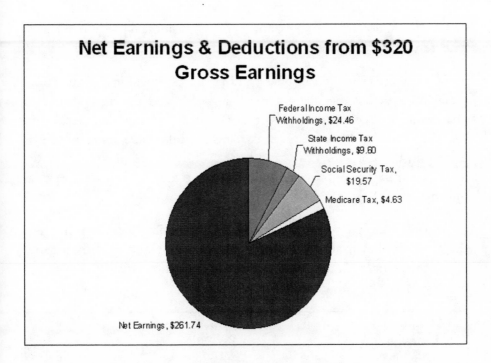

Net Earnings & Deductions from $320 Gross Earnings

Federal Income Tax Withholdings, $24.46

State Income Tax Withholdings, $9.60

Social Security Tax, $19.57

Medicare Tax, $4.63

Net Earnings, $261.74

In the majority of cases, your employer is required by law to deduct tax from your gross earnings and send it to the government. The exception to this requirement is when you file with the Federal Government to be *exempt* from federal taxes. Typically, claiming you are exempt and having no taxes withheld from each paycheck is not recommended because if you end up owing tax at the end of the year, it may be difficult come up with a lump sum required to pay all at once. On the other hand, if you pay more tax than required in any given year, you will receive a refund when you file your tax return. Taxes deducted from your gross earnings include federal income tax (for the U.S. government), and depending on where you live, could include state and city income taxes as well.

Some employers offer or require their employees to have a bank account into which employees' earnings can be directly deposited. This is called "direct deposit" and is both convenient for the employee, because it saves them from having to go to the bank, and the employer, which saves the expense of having to process and mail paper checks. With direct deposit, the employee may receive a paper or electronic pay stub containing the same information as the ones attached to traditional paper paychecks, which we describe below.

When you receive a traditional paper paycheck, it will include two documents: the actual check and a check stub. Most of the time, these two documents are separated by perforation so you can tear the check from the stub. You should take the check to your bank where you can cash or deposit it, but don't forget to keep the stub for your records. By the way, don't toss your pay stub in the trash because it contains valuable personal information.

Below is a sample pay stub from XYZ Corporation. Keep in mind that the tax rates shown are for example purposes only and don't necessarily reflect the actual tax rates. Also, additional deductions may apply, but are not considered for this example.

XYZ Corporation 123 General Road Anytown, USA			Earnings Statement Pay Period: 1/1/07—1/15/07	
John Doe: Social Security #: 111-222-3333			Federal Exemptions: 1 State Exemptions: 1	
Earnings:	Rate 8.00	Hours 40	Gross Earnings 320	Year to Date 320
Deductions:				
	Federal Income Tax		24.46	
	State Income Tax		9.60	
	Social Security Tax		19.57	
	Medicare Tax		4.63	
NET EARNINGS: 261.74				

As you can see, the pay stub will include the name of your employer, your name, and your Social Security number. The pay stub will normally show the dates considered for the pay, known as the pay period. The gross earnings are determined by multiplying the number of hours worked (in this case, 40 hours) by the hourly rate ($8.00 per hour), which equals

$320. Subsequent pay stubs would show a different number in the "Year To Date" section, as this is the running total of all your earnings for a given calendar year.

Federal income tax is the amount deducted for the U.S. government income tax. Likewise, state income tax is the amount deducted for income tax for the state in which you work, assuming your state charges income tax. This example does not include local taxes, which could be deducted depending on the city in which you live.

The federal and state exemptions listed on your pay stub determine how much tax is deducted from your paycheck. Generally, the higher the number of exemptions you claim, the lower your tax deduction. In most cases, a teenager will have one exemption for both federal and state. However, if you were married, your exemptions would climb to two, and if you were married with a child, your exemptions would be three. The basic idea behind exemptions is that you pay a portion of your earnings to taxes from every paycheck so you don't have a large tax bill at the end of the year when you file your tax return. We'll discuss more about exemptions below in the W-4 section.

Social Security tax is a fixed percentage of your income that goes to the Social Security system. Social Security is a U.S. government program for retirement savings. The premise of Social Security is that a person pays into an account throughout their working lives and then receives benefits from the program during retirement. Currently, retired individuals are being paid benefits by those still in the nation's workforce, and those people currently paying into Social Security will receive their benefits from the next generation of workers. Sometimes Social Security tax will be shown on your pay stub as OASDI (Old Age Survivors and Disabilities Act) or FICA (Federal Insurance Contribution Act).

Medicare tax is a deduction for the government health insurance plan for people over the age of 65, although younger people may qualify. Similar to Social Security, Medicare is a government program that offers health benefits to aging Americans.

The W-4 Form

When you accept a job, your employer will provide you with paperwork to be completed prior to starting your position. One of these forms is called the "W-4" from the Internal Revenue Service. According to the IRS, the purpose of the W-4 form is so "your employer can withhold the correct Federal income tax."

The W-4 has several sections of required information but is very simple to complete. On the first page of the W-4 form, there is a worksheet called the "Personal Allowances Worksheet." We won't discuss the details of the form because it won't relate to most teenagers, but the first three items of the worksheet may apply and include the following:

A Enter "1" for yourself if no one else can claim you as a dependent
B Enter "1" if: You are single and have only one job; or
          You are married, have only one job, and your spouse doesn't work
          Your wages from a second job are $1,000 or less
C Enter "1" for your spouse
.

.

H Add lines A through G and enter total here

Lines D through G that are not listed above relate primarily to workers with children and are not covered here. We realize that some teenagers have children, but a majority of people under the age of 18 do not. If you have children, review the additional rows on your W-4, and you will find that the instructions are very easy to follow.

In most cases, teenagers with a job will still be claimed as a dependent on their parents' tax returns. Therefore, most teenagers would not enter "1" for line A. A teenager who is not married would enter "1" for line B, as would a teenager who is married, but only if his or her spouse doesn't work. Therefore, a majority of teenagers would only enter "1" in line H, which is the sum of lines A through G.

The next section of the W-4 is called "Employee's Withholding Allowance Certificate." This is the portion of the form that you complete and return to your employer. This section includes your name, address,

Social Security number, and marital status. Line five of this section asks you to enter the total number of allowances you are claiming from line H of the Personal Allowances Worksheet. Although rare for teenagers, there is a line on this form that allows you to pay additional taxes above those calculated for your exemptions. Finally, you must sign and date the form and return it to your employer.

The hard part is over. You have landed a job, learned how to fill out your W-4 form, and you understand your paycheck. Now let's talk about your hard-earned money.

What Should I Do
with My Money?

Spend, spend, and spend some more. That's what most people do with their money. In fact, most people spend money they don't even have by borrowing money on a credit card, car loan, or other debt. We certainly don't recommend spending everything you earn, much less spending more than you earn. But we realize that you are going to spend some of your money—or why would you go to work in the first place? Saving a portion of the money you make for a nice reward, like an MP3 player, a down payment on a car, or the newest X-Box game may keep you motivated to continue earning money. But as we mentioned above, controlling how much you spend and putting the rest to work for you is the key to financial independence.

Where am I going to keep the money I pay to myself?

Unless you are paid in cash or your earnings are deposited directly into your bank account, you need a way to turn the piece of paper that your paycheck is printed on into actual money. Just because your employer gives you a paycheck doesn't mean that you have that money in your possession. Your employer keeps that money in their bank account until you actually cash or deposit your check. Keep in mind that most paychecks come with a six-month expiration date, so don't collect paychecks—get your money as soon as you can. We're not talking about running out to turn your check into cold, hard cash (although, it sometimes feels nice to wrap your hands around a wad of bills). We are talking about a place that will take your paycheck and handle the transfer of money from your employer to you: a bank.

Banking

If you don't have a bank account yet, it is time to get one. There are more than ten million American families without a single bank account. Banks of various sizes are scattered around most cities. You can't drive more than a few miles in most places without passing at least one bank.

There are dozens of types of bank accounts available to you. Until you're eighteen, however, you need an adult sponsor to open an account for you. The account can be in your name and you can make transactions such as writing checks, making deposits or using the automated teller machine (ATM). Before we discuss which type of bank account is right for you, let's review what types of accounts are available so you can make an educated decision on where to keep your money, and how to successfully manage those accounts.

Let's start with the basics of what you need when you start …

Checking Accounts

A checking account is the most common type of account offered by traditional banking institutions. As the name implies, this is the account that you draw checks from and usually where your ATM withdrawals debit. Basically, a checking account is a conduit for your income, expenditures, and savings.

There are several different types of checking accounts:

- **Basic:** A basic checking account is generally for little more than bill paying and daily expenses. Normally, there is no minimum balance required and money in the account does not earn interest.

- **Interest-bearing:** Interest-bearing checking accounts normally require the customer to keep a minimum balance in order to qualify for interest payments. Additionally, the interest rate may vary depending on the average monthly balance of the account. Similar to a basic account, this account can be used for daily expenditures, but with certainty that the balance will not fall below the threshold for interest payments.

- **Joint:** A joint checking account can be any variation of account options, with two or more people having equal access to the funds in the account.

- **Express:** Express accounts normally require the account holder to perform all banking transactions via an ATM, telephone, or the Internet. Fees may be associated with visiting a banking teller. Express accounts generally have the lowest fees available and low minimum balance requirements.

- **Lifeline:** Checking accounts designed for low-income consumers, lifeline accounts are required by law in Illinois, Massachusetts, Minnesota, New Jersey, New York, Rhode Island and Vermont. Lifeline accounts generally have very low fees, which are controlled by state law.

- **Senior/Student:** Many banks offer special checking account deals for students as well as individuals classified as seniors (over 60 years of age). These special accounts are generally analogous to basic checking accounts with decreased fees for the special classifications.

- **Money Market:** Although a money market account can be classified as a checking account, there are transaction limitations and high minimum balance requirements that would keep a money market account from being a person's primary checking account. Additional information on money market accounts is included in the following section.

Savings Accounts

Banks normally offer two kinds of savings accounts: passbook and statement. Each type of account pays interest to encourage people to keep and accumulate money in the account. You are allowed to make deposits and withdrawals with savings accounts, such as account transfers and ATM withdrawals, but you can't write checks. Savings accounts usually pay lower interest rates than money market accounts or *CDs* (Certificates of Deposit), but pay higher interest rates than interest-bearing checking accounts.

Below is a brief review of the two different types of savings accounts:

- **Statement Savings:** This is the most common type of savings account because it requires the lowest maintenance of the two. Similar to a checking account, the bank will mail a *statement* showing all of the transactions in the account and the current balance on a monthly or quarterly basis. Statement savings accounts generally have a minimum balance requirement, but this can be as low as $5.

- **Passbook Savings:** Passbook savings is an older type of savings account, rarely used anymore. We mention passbook savings in the event that your banking institution still provides such accounts. All transactions in the passbook savings account (withdrawals, normal deposits, and interest deposits) are logged in a booklet. The bank initially provides this booklet, but the account holder keeps the booklet and updates it as appropriate. If the booklet is lost or stolen, the bank will typically charge a fee for replacement. Passbook savings accounts, similar to statement savings accounts, generally have a minimum balance requirement.

Money Market Accounts

More formally known as a money market deposit account, a money market account is similar to a savings account but has limited transaction privileges. Although the transaction limitations can vary, they are generally limited to six transfers or withdrawals per month with no more than three check transactions written against the account. Money market accounts generally have higher minimum balance requirements than savings accounts. Because of the limited transactions, the interest rate paid on a money market account is usually higher than a savings account.

There are three types of money market accounts:

- **Basic:** Normally requires minimum opening deposit of $100

- **Tiered:** Requires a larger opening deposit amount than a basic account but pays a higher yield as deposits increase. For example, an account holder may earn 2.5 percent interest with a $500 balance, but as much as 5 percent interest with a balance of $25,000.

- **Packaged:** Offers a money market account along with savings, CDs and other bank investments. Banks may offer a higher yield to holders of packaged accounts because the account holder is utilizing several different banking services.

Because there are several different types of money market accounts and each type has different minimum balances and fees, you must do your homework to find the correct money market account for you. Some helpful questions to ask of financial institutions include:

- What interest rate does the account pay?

- Is there a monthly maintenance fee?

- What is the minimum opening deposit?

- Is there a fee if my balance drops below the required minimum?

- What is the fee for additional transactions above the allowed number?

- What is the fee for using ATMs?

- What are the differences between types of money market accounts?

- What is the benefit of a packaged money market account?

Brokerage Account

Although brokerage accounts are mainly for investing in stocks, bonds and mutual funds—which we will discuss later—most large brokerages now offer banking services. Again, you must be eighteen years old to hold your own brokerage account, but most brokers will provide a "custodial account," which is an account established by an adult for the benefit of a minor.

A broker is a person or company authorized to buy and sell financial instruments, such as stocks, bonds, and mutual funds. There are three primary types of brokerages: full-service, discount, and on-line. The differences between these types of brokerages are the various services provided and cost.

Full-Service Brokers:
Full-service brokers, as the name implies, provide the most services of the brokerage options. They may call you with stock ideas based on extensive research from their analysis department. They will also frequently review your portfolio to recommend changes in your investing strategy. Because of the services provided, full-service brokers are the most expensive. They will either charge you fees for each transaction, or charge a flat percentage fee of your total portfolio value. Some of the larger full-service brokerages include Morgan Stanley, Solomon Smith Barney, and Merrill Lynch.

Discount Brokers:
Discount brokers are agencies that place buy and sell orders for you, but do not provide the services of a full-service brokerage. You are responsible for keeping track of your investments and doing research on companies of interest. Discount brokers usually have research reports available to you, but it is your responsibility to wade through the information for the pertinent data. Because fewer services are offered from discount brokerages, the costs are less, averaging about $30 for each trade, which is approximately one-half to one-third the price of full-service brokers. Common discount brokers include Charles Schwab and Fidelity.

On-line Brokers:
On-line brokers are simply web sites that allow you to buy and sell securities. You never have human interaction with on-line brokers, and the only service provided by on-line brokers is the ability to trade securities. Companies such as E-Trade and Ameritrade specialize in on-line trading, with transaction prices ranging from $10 to $20.

You don't have to select just one type of broker. You could have brokerage accounts of each different type, and it is also becoming more common for the full-service brokerages to offer some form of discount or on-line options. We'll discuss later which type of brokerage account might be right for you.

Online Banking

It used to be that banking customers had to go inside banks and wait in lines in the lobby or in their cars on the drive-up tellers. Although some people still like interacting with a bank teller in person, the development of online banking has eliminated the need to wait in lines, either inside the bank lobby or in your car.

Online banking allows you to sit at home (or anywhere else that has Internet connectivity) to access your bank accounts 24 hours a day, any day of the week. With online banking, you can transfer funds from one account to another, check your account balances, verify transactions, pay bills, and even allocate funds for investments in CDs, stocks, bonds, or mutual funds.

Traditionally, a person would establish a bank account with an institution located near their home or place of work. If you had to visit the bank regularly, you wanted a bank conveniently located. With online banking, you can now have a bank account located anywhere in the United States. All of your banking can be done "virtually," including establishing the account. This allows you to shop around for the bank that best fits your needs, whether that depends on fees, services, or minimum initial deposits or balances.

Although the options for online banking vary from bank to bank, you can generally count on the following services to be available online from most:

- Verify account balances

- View account transaction details

- Verify status of loans

- Transfer funds between accounts

- Apply for loans

- Pay bills electronically

- Trade stocks or other investments

- Track investment performance

- Download account information

Because online banking is more cost effective for banks, these accounts will generally have lower fees for customers. The convenience of online banking combined with lower fees results in some good incentives for establishing an online bank account. To enjoy the benefits of online banking you need to own or have access to a computer with Internet access. A limitation of online banking is the reliability of the Internet networks and bank servers. Although network failures are rare, they do occur, and during a time of network trouble, you may not have access to your online accounts.

Balancing Accounts

When you pay cash for something and receive change, do you count the change to make sure you received the correct amount? Most people would answer "yes," yet why do so many people ignore keeping track of the balances of their bank accounts? If you don't know how much money you have, it is impossible to know how much you can spend, and how much you need to save to reach your goals.

Below are a few exercises that should help keep track of your bank accounts, and will eventually become second nature in balancing your accounts:

1. **Review your statement:** This sounds very obvious to most people, but we've seen people with piles of unopened bank statements for months of transactions. Open your bank statements as soon as you get them and compare them to your check register. Notify your bank immediately of anything that looks unusual.

2. **Use technology:** Although your money is considered safe in a bank, it is still your obligation to make sure the banking records are accurate. A monthly review is important, but with the technology available today, you should review your accounts more often. Take advantage of online or telephone access to your accounts so you know the current status of balances, outstanding checks, and

other transactions. Not only will this help you avoid fees, but it will also alert you to abnormal activity.

3. **Understand the fees:** When you read your monthly statements, pay attention to the fees associated with writing checks, using the ATM or teller, or using your debit card. Planning your transactions to avoid these fees can help to maintain your balance over time so you aren't paying unnecessary and excessive fees.

4. **Record transactions immediately:** This process is fairly easy when writing checks but becomes more difficult when using a debit card or ATM. Get in the habit of immediately recording transactions in your check register, and it will be easier to balance your accounts and accurately keep track of where you are spending your money.

5. **Use carbon copies:** Carbon copies are an instant record of all the checks you write, which simplifies tracking your check expenditures.

6. **Use cash:** Using cash for small purchases such as gas, lunch, or other daily expenditures can minimize the number of transactions and make balancing your accounts easier. Make sure you keep your receipts so that you can track your cash purchases ... another handy way to do this is just keep a small pocket pad with you all the time and write down how you spend the cash—it's easy.

7. **Use overdraft protection:** Many banks will allow you to link your checking account with your savings account so that money will automatically be transferred to your checking account if there isn't enough money to cover a transaction. This can help avoid overdraft fees. However, most banks limit the number of automatic transfers each month.

Action Plan

If you don't have a bank account yet, it is time to get one. Look around your neighborhood to see which banks are convenient for you, or which ATMs won't charge you fees if you bank with a certain institution. Ask your parents where they bank and why they bank there. Shop around at different banks for the best deal. Find out who has the lowest minimum balance, fewest fees, highest interest rates, etc. Be sure to take advantage of your student status to get a student account.

Once you have checking and savings accounts, start putting all of your money into your accounts. Break open your piggy bank and take the money to the bank. Your money certainly isn't growing if it is stuck inside a piggy bank. Figure out how much money you will need for the next month of expenses and keep that amount in your checking account. Transfer the rest into your savings account and don't be tempted to transfer it back for additional purchases. The money in your savings account is for saving, so you should think of it as off limits for new clothes, the latest CD, or a new hockey stick.

Once you have enough money to begin investing, you need to think about a brokerage account. Again, ask your parents if they have a brokerage account and analyze the option of a custodial account at that firm. Frequently, a custodial account can carry lower fees and lower minimum investments than other options. If you want to go it alone, you can consider an online brokerage account through a company such as E-Trade or Charles Schwab, although you will need a sponsor over the age of eighteen to help you establish the account.

In summary, open a checking and savings account before anything else. Sock away as much money as you can in your savings account by budgeting your monthly expenses through your checking account. When you have enough money to invest, consider opening a brokerage account to access investments, such as those previously described. But prior to opening a brokerage account, read the next few chapters on saving and investing so you have a clear strategy on which investments you prefer and how to access them.

Be Careful with Your Cards

Day-to-day financial transactions are completed more and more frequently with plastic—ATM cards, debit cards, and credit cards. In fact, more than 50 million credit card transactions are completed every day[2]—that's more than 600 per second! Along with the convenience provided by these cards are some scary realities. Protecting your cards and managing how you use them are critical steps in your path toward financial independence.

Typically, when you open a checking or savings account, the bank or financial institution will offer you an ATM card and/or a debit card. Let's first address the ATM card.

ATM machines can be found these days in most places that are frequented by people—grocery stores, gas stations, sports arenas, and just about everywhere in between. Sure, it is convenient to have these machines around, but why do you think they are there? ATM machines exist to make money, not just dispense money. More often than not, when you use an ATM not owned by your bank, your withdrawal will include a "convenience charge." This charge varies from machine to machine, but normally runs between $1.50 and $2.50. However, it is possible that these fees can be as high as $10 or $20. Fortunately, the owner of the ATM is required by law to notify you of the fee prior to completing your transaction, so if you think the fee is too high, cancel your transaction and find a different machine.

---

2   www.bankrate.com

Let's consider an example. Say you go to the ATM to withdraw $20 and the ATM charges you $2 for the "convenience" of using that machine. Two dollars may not seem like much, but it constitutes 10 percent of your transaction! Now assume that you use the ATM twice per week over the course of a year. That amounts to $208 in fees each year. So watch your ATM fees and shop around for a bank that either reimburses you for other company's ATM fees, or has ATM machines with no fees that are convenient for you to use so you aren't tempted to pay additional charges at other ATMs.

Now about debit cards: as much as debit cards look like credit cards, they differ in many ways, not all of which are to your advantage. Typically a debit card carries a logo from a large credit card clearinghouse, such as Visa or MasterCard. But the card can also work as your ATM card, providing cash from an automated teller when you need it. When you access your account via an ATM, you are required to enter your personal identification number (PIN) for security.

When your card is used at the point of sale for merchandise, a PIN is not required. The federal government protects credit cards and any loss due to fraudulent activity is generally limited to $50. Debit cards carry no such protection. If your debit card is lost or stolen and used fraudulently, money can be pulled directly from your account until there is nothing left. Technically, you are responsible for all of the charges.

By law, if your credit card is used fraudulently, you have sixty days to notify the bank and the most you will have to pay is $50 of the total fraudulent transactions. With debit cards, you must notify the bank within two business days in order to limit your loss to $50. If you wait between three and sixty days, you're responsible for up to $500. If you wait longer than sixty days, all bets are off and you may be responsible for every fraudulently spent dollar *and* any additional fees charged for bouncing checks, overdraft transfers, or other penalties.

All cards, whether credit cards, debit cards or ATM cards, must be safeguarded against loss, theft and overuse. However, the use of credit cards must be more closely monitored than ATM and debit cards because they involve the use of money that does not belong to you. If you only have $50 in your bank account, you can't withdrawal $100 with your ATM card. If you reach for your credit card to make a purchase, you are effectively getting a loan from someone else, which carries significant risk.

The Risks of Using Other People's Money

Banks pay you to save money, calling it interest. You may be wondering why someone would be willing to pay you not to spend your own money. If it's your parent, maybe they're willing to pay to teach you a concept or help develop a habit, as we saw in Sean's case. Sean's father paid 10 cents for every dollar his son saved, teaching Sean the power of interest. But what about banks? When you deposit your money in an interest-bearing savings account, for instance, they will pay you a certain amount in interest. What's in it for them?

First, they don't care if you aren't spending your money; they care that your money is in the account so they can "borrow" it from you. They are willing to pay you if they can hold—and use—your money. Why? Because they will turn around and *loan* your money to someone else who needs it. They will pay you a certain amount in interest to "hold" your money for you but will charge the person borrowing the money a greater amount in interest. In other words, the bank, or other institution to which you make a deposit, can loan your money out to other people and charge these borrowers more in interest than they are paying you. The bank then keeps the difference.

This concept is known as the "bank spread," which is the difference between the interest banks pay to their customers and what banks charge to loan money to customers. For example, a bank may pay you three percent interest on your savings account. If you take out a car loan with that same bank, they may charge you interest of 10 percent. Effectively, they are loaning you the money from their customer's savings accounts. In this example, the difference between what the bank charges in interest and pays in interest, or the spread, is seven percent.

In Sean's case, his father may have paid him 10 percent interest while he was turning around and charging his neighbor 15 percent interest to borrow the money he was holding for Sean until Sean asked for it back. In doing so, Sean's father could have made 5 cents on every dollar he loaned the neighbor.

But what if Sean's father paid Sean only three percent to hold his son's money and charged his neighbor 25 percent interest to borrow money? As you can see, creditors, or lenders, can potentially make a lot of money, depending on interest rates.

But because the U.S. is a society of consumers (many of whom don't know the difference between wants and needs), all too often borrowers use other people's money (and pay the associated fees) for the wrong reasons: to acquire the things they *want* but don't really need. Basically, paying a fee to borrow money is the opposite of investing, although in certain circumstances borrowing can be advantageous to the borrower if their money is used for something that *appreciates*, or gains, in value, such as a home in a desirable neighborhood.

Imagine that instead of investing your money you spent it all on things you wanted and needed. Then imagine you found one item you have been wanting for a long time—a new Nintendo Wii that costs $250. You can't pay for the Wii outright, because you don't have enough in your bank account. But you do have a credit card that you got for "free" at a recent concert.

If you purchase the Wii with your new credit card, you can have the game immediately and you only have to pay a minimum amount every month, which you decide you can afford. Sounds like a good deal, right? The only catch is that in addition to coming up with the minimum monthly payment for the Wii, you will also be charged monthly interest on the outstanding balance. You decide that the interest is a price you're willing to pay for the Wii. After all, you've wanted it for a long time and it will make you happy to have it. What harm can be done? You'll pay it off … eventually.

This is exactly what consumer lenders want you to think. The act of purchasing beyond one's means is what keeps them in business. Borrowing money from someone else, whether a bank, credit card company, or individual, almost *always* comes at a cost beyond the price of the good or service purchased. Unfortunately, the cost is all too often much greater than the borrower originally thought. Remember the time value of money? Well, instead of earning money over time with an investment, you will lose money over time by paying interest on consumer debt. If you pay the minimum monthly payment, you will actually pay more in interest than the original cost of the Wii. Plus, because that money is being paid to someone else, it can't be invested and earning interest for you. Is it really worth it? If your credit card charges 24 percent interest, as many do, that $250 Wii could cost you $500 over three years if you just pay the minimum monthly payment.

In a nation that is virtually saturated with advertisements, there is an ever-growing population of buyers that cannot say "no" and that are unwilling or unable to discern between needs and wants. They want to live like their friends or neighbors who drive new SUVs and travel every other month, so they buy freely, saddle themselves with debt, and lose their financial independence. A lost job, serious illness, or other financial bump in the road is all it takes to bring the whole house of cards tumbling down. And then what? The bank forecloses on the house, the car dealer repossess the car, the family declares bankruptcy and starts from square one, only this time with a stained financial history and without their most valuable asset: time.

We don't want to sound like we're on a soapbox, but one of the largest contributors to financial problems in the United States is the personal credit card. Although convenient, credit cards can lead to disastrous spending patterns because every time you use your credit card, you are taking out a loan that must be repaid. So, if you are going to use a credit card, it is imperative that you know how to use it wisely.

How Can I Use a Credit Card Wisely?

By now you have probably noticed that cash is being used less and less for everyday transactions. If you're in a hurry to make a purchase, you may remember a time when you were frustrated at the sight of the person in front of you counting bills or writing a check for their purchase. More commonly, people just pull out their credit card, swipe it through a small machine, sign for their goods and go on their way. Some transactions like renting a car or buying things on line may require a credit card.

Whether you want a credit card for convenience or you think it is an absolute necessity to function in today's society, we will give you some ideas for using your plastic wisely.

First of all, be responsible with your credit card. Although you aren't pulling cash out of your pocket when you use your credit card, visualize that you are. Recognize that the money you're spending is real money, and don't get carried away with your credit limit if it is higher than what you can afford to repay, which is commonly the case.

Next, carry only one credit card. Establish a pattern of making small purchases on your credit card and paying the balance in full every month. If you have more than one credit card, it may get confusing to keep track of how much you have spent on each card and your spending can quickly spiral out of control.

Third, budget your money *before* you spend with your credit card. Don't get caught in the trap of buying something on impulse that you can't pay for when the bill comes. Know how much you can afford (i.e. how much you have budgeted in your checking account) before you even consider pulling out your plastic. Many credit card companies provide online access to track spending. Don't wait until your statement arrives to view your transactions. You don't want to be surprised that you blew your monthly budget.

Fourth, pay your credit card bill before the due date and pay your balance in full each month. Paying your credit card bill late, even by one day, can cost you a lot of money in additional fees and will adversely affect your credit rating. If you don't pay off your full balance each month, you will be subject to interest on your balance and it becomes more difficult to keep within your budget. Credit card companies charge interest based on the average daily balance of the account. If you charge $100 on the first day of your billing cycle and then submit a payment of $50 when your statement arrives, you will be charged interest on the full $100. Now you owe more than $50 next month, even if you don't make additional purchases. If you pay the full amount due—$100 in this example—your interest payment will be zero.

Finally, beware of the minimum monthly payment trap. When you get your credit card bill, you will see, in bold numbers, the minimum monthly payment due. To avoid this trap, ignore this section of the bill. The credit card company is trying to get you to pay very little on your balance so they can charge you interest on the remaining balance in subsequent months. In fact, by only paying the minimum amount due, it could take years to eliminate a sizable balance while monthly interest fees continue to add up.

Credit cards can offer you many conveniences with financial transactions and can help you build a personal credit record. But many people believe that credit cards are the single worst offender in leading to debt, credit, and overall financial problems for millions of Americans. Use your credit cards wisely and be responsible with your purchases.

What You Don't Know
Can Hurt You

When I first got my credit card, I was very proud of it and loved using it for everything from movies to downloading songs on the Internet. I guess it was somewhat of a status symbol for me. I recognized that I could get in trouble by spending more than I was capable of paying, since the credit card gave me a spending limit of $5,000.

Although I couldn't pay off the balance in full every single month, I tried my best and paid as much as I could, making sure my payment arrived on time. I knew that eventually I would pay off the balance in full, and my credit card only had an interest rate of 12 percent. One particular month during final exams, I forgot about my credit card bill and noticed it just two days before the bill was due. I quickly wrote a check and put it in the mail.

I was shocked when I received my next statement showing a $50 late fee and a new interest rate of 32 percent. My check arrived one day after the due date. Now it was going to be very difficult for me to pay off my credit card, not to mention the $50 that I basically gave away by not paying attention. After calling the credit card company, I was told that the documentation that arrived with my card contained the "small print" explaining what would happen if my payment was even a day late. I'm currently looking for a new credit card company, and I'll be sure that I never miss a payment deadline again. Maybe I should have paid more attention to the fine print before I started using my credit card.

—Jonathan, 17, Los Angeles, CA

Many people end up in financial trouble because they fail to read—or heed—the small print on things like loan documents and credit card agreements. Why do you think the print is so small? Are the companies trying to use less paper to save money or be environmentally sensitive? Don't think so. They want as few people as possible to read their documents so that consumers unknowingly violate the rules, which justifies the credit card company (or other lender) in jacking up the interest rate. "Zero percent interest, no annual fee"—sounds like a great deal! In the small print: "Miss a payment by a day and you pay 32 percent interest on all outstanding balances, and if your payment to *another* credit card company is late, your interest rate on *this* card will increase to 32 percent." It happens all the time.

Listen, we are not saying that all credit card companies and lenders are purposely deceiving their customers. Most of these companies are very ethical and only applying penalties to the people who represent the highest risk of not paying their bills. We make this illustration not to give the lending industry a black-eye, but to help you realize the importance of understanding the terms of your agreement and making the necessary payments on time.

Investing: It Takes Money
to Make Money

Investing is about making money. More specifically, investing is about making the money that you earned more valuable for you over time so that you can reach your financial goals, like being a millionaire, paying for college, driving a Ferrari, or whatever.

The term "investing" means different things to different people. Some people may say they "invested" in a house just to have a place to live. Others may say they "invested" in a new car because it looks cool, or they "invested" in an expensive leather jacket because everyone else has one. This kind of investing implies that that a person is putting money toward an item in the hope that it will appreciate in value. Investing does not mean spending! An investment is a temporary activity (meaning not permanent) in which something of value (usually money) is applied to a risk instrument that is expected—but not necessarily guaranteed—to increase in value over time.

Buying consumer goods, such as a car or a leather jacket, is spending. Once you consume the product (drive the car or wear the jacket), the value of the good is less than what you paid for it. The process of something losing value is known as *depreciation*—the opposite of appreciation. So even if you can sell it at a later date, the value of the item will not make up for the money you spent to acquire it. However, buying a house can be an investment, assuming that you are buying it with the hope that the worth of the home will increase—or appreciate in value—while you're living in it. In this case, you are investing in a home rather than spending money to simply acquire something you want.

Investing vs. Saving

Investing also has distinctly separate connotations from saving. Saving implies that you are accumulating a certain amount of something, like money in a piggy bank. At some point, you can apply your piggy bank savings to investments, but the money you are saving is *not* necessarily an investment.

The key difference between saving and investing is *rate of return*. The amount of money you make on an investment in relation to the amount of time your money is involved in the investment is the rate of return. When you make an investment, you are hoping that when you sell or exit the investment, you will have more money than when you started.

Assume that you have $100 per month, or $1,200 per year of extra cash. You can either save it under your mattress or invest it. In the table below, you will find how the rate of return (compounded monthly) will affect your investment dollars while not impacting your savings:

$1,200 per year: Investing vs. Saving

Year	Savings No rate of return	Investment With 4% rate of return	Investment With 7% rate of return	Investment With 10% rate of return
1	$1,200	$1,222	$1,239	$1,256
5	$6,000	$6,630	$7,159	$7,744
10	$12,000	$14,725	$17,308	$20,484
20	$24,000	$36,677	$52,092	$75,937

As you can see, the rate of return on investments significantly increases the value of your money over time. Furthermore, the example does not include the cost of inflation, which causes your money in savings to have *less* purchasing power in the future than it does today because prices for consumer goods like gas, clothes, and food go up over time. Therefore, money in non-interest-bearing accounts, such as most checking accounts, actually *loses* value over time, while investments increase in value.

If your parents own their own home, they probably consider it an investment. We previously discussed the differences between saving and investing, including some common misconceptions about investments. Now, we will give you some information about *equity investments,* particularly stocks, bonds, and mutual funds. Later we will give you some strategies for starting out, but first review the following section to familiarize yourself with these investment vehicles.

Stocks

A stock is a piece of paper that represents part ownership in a company. Companies issue stock to raise money, which the company can use for a variety of purposes such as research and development, opening a new factory, or hiring more workers. In order to raise money, a company either has to borrow it from a lender or sell a part of the company in the form of *stock shares*. If you become a *stockholder*, you become part owner of the company issuing the stock. Stocks are bought and sold or "traded" on a *stock exchange* such as the New York Stock Exchange (NYSE).

Consequently, as a stockholder you have the right to vote on the direction of the company. Because most individual stockowners have very little percentage ownership in a company, one individual investor (or stockholder) can rarely directly affect how a company does business. Therefore, the art to picking stocks is to find companies with good track records and a high probability for improving their earnings. When a company's earnings improve, the value of the company increases, and investors are willing to pay more for the stock, which increases the stock price. When the stock price goes up, the individual stockholders can make money—if they sell the stock—because the new price is higher than the price at which the investor originally purchased shares of stock.

Stocks have been solid investments in recent history. As the economy grows, corporate earnings increase, and stock prices climb. In fact, over the past thirty years, the average large stock has had an average return of more than 10 percent per year[3]. This represents significant growth in the value of stock investments. During that time, however, the stock market has also been through a dozen *bear markets* (average total stock value decline of more than 20 percent). If a person invested at the wrong time during this period, they could suffer considerable loss in the value of their investment.

Therefore, successful stock investing is a long-term endeavor. Although we hear stories of investors reaping huge rewards for short-term, risky investments, the strategy of "buy-and-hold" over a long time period is the safest stock investment strategy. It is important to remember that investments, including those in the stock market, involve risk and do not guarantee a positive return just because they have performed well in the past.

History of the Dow:

What does it mean when you flip on the television and see the news report that the Dow Jones Industrial Average (also known as the DJIA, Dow Jones, or Dow) was up 2 percent or down 50 points?

The Dow Jones Industrial Average is the oldest measure of the U.S. stock market and the most widely used indicator of stock market activity. In 1884, a journalist named Charles H. Dow invented a way to follow the overall activity of the stock market on a daily basis. He put together a list of twelve important stocks and at the end of each trading session, added up all their prices at the day's end and divided by 12. This gave him an average share price for the 12 important stocks, which he published in a news bulletin.

Eventually, this average became known as the Dow Jones Industrial Average after one of Charles Dow's colleagues named Jones provided

---

3   http://money.cnn.com

some assistance on tracking the average. The DJIA has been utilized in the investment community for tracking stocks—and an indicator of the overall health of the nation's economy—for more than a century. Today, when people ask, "What's up with the stock market today?" or "Where did the market close?" they often are talking about the DJIA.

The original DJIA was made up of twelve companies. As the economy expanded, eighteen more companies were added. The stocks tracked by the DJIA are constantly changing due to mergers, acquisitions, and changes in the economy. The stocks that make up the DJIA are chosen quarterly or annually as representative of the broad market and of American industries. The companies selected are considered to be major players in their respective industries and their stock is widely held by individual and institutional investors. The DJIA is solely comprised of stocks traded on the NYSE.

The Standard & Poor's 500 (S&P 500) is another index similar to the DJIA. This index consists of 500 stocks selected based on market size and industry group representation. A majority of stocks in the S&P 500 are traded on the NYSE, while smaller portions are traded on a stock exchange called the National Association of Securities Dealers Automated Quotations, or "NASDAQ."

Why does a company like Microsoft® sell shares of itself to ordinary investors? As mentioned previously, selling shares is a way for a company to raise money to buy a new building, hire more employees, or fund a large marketing campaign. Typically, the decision to sell shares of a company is made before a company is the size of Microsoft. In fact, many people contend that Microsoft, and most of the other large companies in the world, would not be that large without selling shares. When a company initially sells shares of itself, it is referred to as the *Initial Public Offering* or "going public." The company offers shares of the company for sale to the public in the form of stock that trades on a stock exchange.

The Initial Public Offering

The initial offer of shares on a stock exchange is called the Initial Public Offering (IPO), and the proceeds from the stock sales go the company's bank account, although the firms who help a company go public (investment banks, accountants and attorneys) take a healthy fee.

The new shareholders of the company now own a piece of the business, but the issuing company normally maintains a majority stake (at least 51 percent) so they can still control voting rights.

Stock Price Fluctuation

After the Initial Public Offering, the stock of the company trades on a stock exchange, such as the NYSE or the NASDAQ. The purpose of these exchanges is to match buyers of stock with sellers. Based upon supply and demand, the prices of stocks on the market continually fluctuate. If there are no sellers of a particular stock that a buyer wants, he or she will raise the offer price until someone is willing to sell. On the other hand, if there are few buyers for a certain stock and many sellers, the buyers will reduce the amount they are willing to pay for a share of stock.

When researching a stock, you will notice three different prices associated with one share: bid, ask, and current. The bid price is the most amount of money per share that a buyer is willing to pay for the stock. The ask price is the lowest amount of money per share that a seller is willing to get from selling the stock. The current price is the dollar amount associated with one share of stock. The current price is always fluctuating from a few cents to several dollars or more. These fluctuations are based upon the volume of shares being traded and the bid and ask prices. When a buyer's bid price matches a sellers ask price, the transaction takes place.

Mutual Funds

A mutual fund is a collection of financial securities (stocks, bonds, cash, real estate, etc.) managed by a person or company on behalf of multiple investors. The person or company responsible for the management of the fund, called the *fund manager*, sells shares in the fund to individual investors. The fund manager makes investment decisions with the "pool" of money from all the investors and keeps track of the holdings.

Many mutual funds allow you to start investing with very little money, so you can have a diverse collection of investments without separately investing in many different securities. The cost of this collection of investments, or *portfolio*, may also be less than if you were to purchase individual stocks separately because a mutual fund invests in many stocks with only one transaction price, or *load fee*, versus dozens of transaction fees incurred in individual stock trades.

Net Asset Value

Since a mutual fund may have hundreds or thousands of individual investors who buy and sell the fund everyday, a concept called *Net Asset Value* is used to determine the price for a share in the fund. *Net Asset Value* (NAV) is the total value of the securities in the fund divided by the number of shares owned by investors. Generally, the fund manager will calculate NAV every day and investors can either buy or sell shares of the fund at that daily price. Since NAV is calculated every day, this type of mutual fund is commonly called an *open-ended fund*.

Mutual funds have become the most popular equity investment for a variety of reasons, including:

- **Diversification:** A mutual fund can contain securities from many different sources (possibly even hundreds or thousands), which most individual investors can't afford to do separately. Diversification reduces the risk for loss when a particular industry or company has financial problems. However, don't assume that all mutual funds are diversified. Mutual funds have become so popular that there are now very specific mutual funds that invest in specialized industries or even countries.

- **Liquidity:** Mutual fund shares can be bought and sold on any business day, so investors have quick access to cash. With individual stocks, a stock seller must be matched to a corresponding stock buyer for the transaction to occur. If no buyers exist to offset the seller, you may not be able to turn your stock investment into cash immediately.

- **Convenience:** Mutual funds have many conveniences available. You can invest in a mutual fund that supports your beliefs, such as investing in only environmentally friendly companies or companies in a particular geography. Additionally, fund managers usually make investing in mutual funds easy through automatic investment options, such as transferring $100 every month directly from your checking account, and provide detailed paperwork for tracking performance and filing taxes.

- **Management:** Certified professionals manage mutual funds. Since most of us are not stock market experts, we don't have the time to manage our investments on a daily basis. Investing in a mutual fund employs the expertise of a professional, who uses extensive research, market information, and industry experts, to make the right investment decisions on behalf of you and the mutual fund's other shareholders.

Mutual funds come in all shapes and sizes. Below are some of the most common types of mutual funds available:

- **Value Funds:** Managers of value funds attempt to invest in stocks that have become "undervalued," or have low prices relative to their earning potential. For a variety of reasons, the manager believes the stock price will rise from its current price. Stocks in value funds come from either large companies that are selling at discounts to their peer groups, or small companies that the manager believes have been missed by investors.

- **Growth Funds:** As the name implies, growth fund managers try to invest in stocks of growing companies. For the most part, growth funds focus on companies with market momentum, or considerable recent price appreciation. Because growth funds try to capitalize on the current trend of the market, they carry higher risk than value funds, but also provide the opportunity for higher return.

- **Specialty Funds:** Specialty funds concentrate their assets on certain sectors or specialties. Specialty funds range from broad funds, such as a fund that invests in Latin American companies, to detailed funds, which could invest only in things such as value-based Internet firms, health care companies, real estate investments, etc. Specialty funds are appropriate for investors who want to direct their money to a particular industry or geography without buying individual stocks in that sector.

- **Balanced (or Blended) Funds:** Balanced funds are generally the lowest risk mutual funds available. They provide for long-term growth, but also *balance* their investments with income opportunities through dividends and/or bonds. Balanced funds will drop less in value than the overall market in difficult financial times, but will also appreciate less than the overall market during a rally.

- **Index Funds:** An index fund invests in all of the particular companies of a tracking index, such as the S&P 500. An S&P 500 index fund, for example, invests in the stocks of the 500 companies that comprise the index. The fund manager of an index fund doesn't worry about which stocks to invest in because he or she only invests in the stocks included in the index. Since index funds require no research or sophisticated stock analysis, they are usually the cheapest funds to invest in.

Bonds

When you invest in stocks and mutual funds, you are buying partial ownership of the company or companies issuing the stock. When you invest in a bond, you are loaning money for a certain time period to the issuer, which could be the U.S. government, a state, a local municipality or a large company like General Motors. The government issues bonds to raise money to build roads and schools. Large companies issue bonds to build new factories. Like any loan, the borrower will pay interest on the loan, which is income to bond holders.

When you buy a bond, the price you pay is called the *face value*. The bond issuer promises to pay back your investment on a particular day in the future, called the *maturity date*. During the time you hold the bond, you will receive interest payments, called the *coupon*. For instance, a bond with a $1,000 face value (the cost to buy the bond), a 5 percent coupon (the interest) and a 10-year maturity would pay you $50 a year for ten years. At the end of the ten years, you would receive your $1,000 back.

Bonds are known as *fixed-income* investments because, as the example above shows, the amount of return is fixed and will not fluctuate based on economic factors.

Similar to mutual funds, bonds are available in many different forms, including:

- **United States Government Bonds (Treasuries):** U.S. Government bonds include Treasury Bills, Treasury Notes, and Treasury Bonds. Treasuries are regarded as the safest bond investments because they are backed by "the full faith and credit" of the U.S. Government.

  o **Treasury Bills (or T-bills):** T-bills are short-term treasuries with maturities ranging from 90 days to one year. You buy them at a discount to their face value and receive the full value at maturity, with the difference being the interest. For example, you might buy a T-bill for $800 that matures in 5 years. After 5 years, you would receive $1,000 back, earning $200 in interest.

  o **Treasury Notes:** Treasury notes mature between two and ten years. Interest is paid twice per year at a fixed rate, with a minimum investment of $1,000.

  o **Treasury Bonds:** Treasury bonds mature between ten and thirty years with semiannual interest payments and a minimum investment of $1,000.

- **Zero-coupon Bonds:** Zero-coupon bonds don't make regular interest payments each year like regular bonds. Rather, the bond is sold at a deep discount and at maturity the holder collects all of the compound interest plus the principle. These bonds are normally held in tax-deferred accounts because the holder must pay tax on the interest annually, even though they don't collect the interest until maturity.

- **Inflation-indexed Treasuries:** Inflation-indexed treasuries pay interest based on the consumer price index (CPI). These treasuries are designed to maintain value regardless of inflationary factors in the economy.

- **Mortgage-backed Bonds:** The government issues mortgage loans through Ginnie Mae, Freddie Mac, and Fannie Mae. We won't go into detail about what these funny names mean, but they are basically federal programs to assist with home buying. Mortgage-backed bonds provide an ownership stake in those loans and earn interest from the borrowers.

- **Municipal Bonds:** Usually issued by state and local governments, municipal bonds mature in one to 40 years and interest payments may be tax deductible. Due to the tax advantages of these bonds, they usually come with lower returns than equivalent taxable bonds.

- **Corporate Bonds:** Corporate bonds pay interest and have maturities that range from a few weeks to 100 years. These bonds carry higher risk than treasuries because companies have been known to go bankrupt, which would eliminate any maturity of the bond. Corporations issuing bonds with low credit quality are called "junk" bonds because of the high inherent risk. Due to this risk, however, investors normally earn higher yields than other types of bonds.

Reading Stock and Mutual Fund Pages

When you thumb through the business section of your local newspaper or browse through a copy of the *Wall Street Journal*, you may notice the multiple pages of small-print stock and mutual fund information.

These pages consist of row after row of information related to nearly every publicly traded stock (at least on the larger exchanges) and popular mutual funds. Each row will start with a name of a stock (usually listed as a "ticker" symbol) or the name of the mutual fund, followed by a series of numbers.

Depending on which financial resource you are using to look at stock or mutual fund performance, the level of detail will vary. The following examples are basic stock and mutual fund reports:

NYSE:	October 25, 2007						
Stock	Close	Change	High	Low	Volume	52-wk Hi	52-wk Low
HPQ	52.51	1.12	52.64	51.96	8.47M	53.00	38.14

This is the actual stock report for Hewlett-Packard Company on October 25, 2007. As you can see, the name of the stock is not listed as Hewlett-Packard because there isn't enough room on all of the stock pages to list each company's full name. Therefore, during the initial public offering process, companies select a "Ticker" symbol that will be used to represent their stock on the stock market. Hewlett-Packard's ticker symbol is HPQ.

At the end of the trading day for Hewlett-Packard, the stock closed at $52.51 per share, reflected above as "Close." The "Change" column is the difference from the previous trading day's close, so Hewlett-Packard stock was up $1.12 from October 24 to the end of trading on October 25, 2007. The "High" and "Low" columns refer to the daily stock peaks and valleys, which can give you an idea of the volatility of the stock. The "Volume" shows how many shares were bought and sold during this particular day. Finally, the "52-week High" and "52-week Low" give you an idea of how the stock is trending by showing you the highest and lowest prices of the stock over the last 52 weeks.

More detailed stock pages will include additional information, such as average daily volume, market capitalization, price-to-earnings ratio, as well as dividend and yield. We won't discuss these items because the example above is the most common and provides the majority of information you will need. Additionally, hundreds of financial web sites exist to provide you with plenty of detailed information on stock quotes, as well as in-depth explanations that pertain to that information.

Now let's examine the mutual fund pages for a sample fund:

Mutual Finals:	October 25, 2007			
Name	NAV	Change	YTD	YTD%
Sample Fund	29.76	+0.05	+9.57	49.32

Fortunately, the mutual fund pages have less information to review and are therefore easier to understand. Similar to the stock pages, the mutual fund pages begin with the mutual fund name. Sometimes the mutual fund names are abbreviated to save newspaper space, but normally the abbreviations are close enough to the actual name for you to understand what they represent.

In the mutual fund section above, we discussed net asset value, which is shown in every mutual fund page, analogous to the price of a stock in our previous example. The "Change" column reflects the amount the NAV changed in the particular day under examination. The "YTD" column shows the change in the NAV since January 1 of the current year, but frequently only the percentage change is noted. The "YTD%" is the percentage change in the value of the mutual fund during the current calendar year. In this example, the mutual fund has increased in value by 49.32 percent. Therefore, had you invested $100 in this fictitious mutual fund on January 1, your investment would be worth $149.32 on October 25, 2007.

Free Money: IRA and 401(k)

Yes, you read it correctly: free money. You are probably a bit suspicious about anything you hear being "free" because nothing really is free. However, with some careful planning and if you invest your money in the right places, you can actually get free money. But be careful how and when you spend this money because in many cases, if you spend it before your retirement, you will face steep penalties and fees.

After reading the last sentence, you may be thinking, "You must be kidding talking about retirement—I'm still living with my parents!" We realize that you are just getting started with your own money and retirement seems an eternity away. But hang with us; we have some compelling reasons to consider an individual retirement account, or IRA, as a teenager. If you are already fortunate enough to work for a company that provides a 401(k) account, you would be wise to take advantage of it.

Individual Retirement Accounts

IRAs are designed to hold investments until retirement. These accounts are similar to regular brokerage accounts, but they have some tax advantages as well as some penalties for not following the IRA rules.

Most people, even teenagers, are eligible to open and invest in IRA accounts through banks, brokerages, and other financial companies. The first rule to investing in IRAs is that you need to have earned income, which is money earned from a job and subject to regular income tax. This means the $50 check you received as a birthday gift from your Aunt Lucy cannot be used to open an IRA unless you have at least $250 of income from employment.

Another rule of an IRA account is that your monetary contribution cannot exceed the maximum amount allotted for the year. In 2007, the maximum was $4,000, increasing to $5,000 in 2008 and beyond. Finally, in order to avoid significant penalties, you must leave your money in your IRA account until you are at least 59 ½ years of age.

There are two main kinds of IRAs: traditional and Roth. Initially, a traditional IRA was known just as an IRA. When the Roth IRA was introduced, the term *traditional* was used to differentiate the two accounts.

Traditional IRA

A traditional IRA is for pretax deposits (or money invested directly from your earned income) and is not subject to income tax. This is also known as *tax deductible* because the savings are realized when you deduct the contribution amount on your annual income tax filing. Investing money before income tax is calculated can be very beneficial to your financial goals. IRA accounts grow tax-deferred until you take money out of the account. In addition, any capital gains that are realized in your account grow tax-free until distribution. The benefit of tax-deferred investing is that when you retire, it is likely that your income tax rate will drop and the tax liability on your investments will be less. There are situations in which contributions to a traditional IRA are not tax deductible, but these limitations are primarily based on the highest income-earning Americans and will not be discussed here.

Roth IRA

A Roth IRA is for post-tax deposits, or money invested after you have paid income tax on your earnings. Although you lose the advantages of pre-tax investment, the Roth IRA allows you to never pay additional tax on the investment money. Investments in a Roth IRA can grow over many years and are not subject to income tax upon distribution, assuming that you keep your investments in your account for a minimum of five years and you don't withdrawal funds prior to 59 ½ years of age. Assuming growth over time, you can see that paying tax on the initial investment dollars of $2,000, for example, would be much less than having to pay tax on the larger amount you withdraw at retirement. Remember the power of compound interest.

Why you, a teenager, should consider an IRA

We know that as a teenager, thinking about being sixty years old happens about as often as thinking about a establishing a petting zoo on the moon. But maybe you will be a little more interested if you consider that investing in an IRA can effectively be free!

What? Free money? Yes! There are, however, requirements to investing in IRAs that provide free money, so don't picture someone just handing out investment accounts or cash at the brokerage. You have to do your part to partake in this free money, and it is called paying taxes.

Let's consider that you work part-time and make $10,000 per year. When you get your paycheck, a certain portion will be deducted for income tax. At the end of the year, your taxable income will be $10,000. Now assume that you have saved $2,000 over the course of the year. If you open a traditional IRA and put that $2,000 into the account, the government will deduct it from your taxable income. Therefore, you will pay income tax on $8,000 instead of $10,000. If you are in the 25 percent tax bracket, your investment results in a tax savings of $500 because by investing in an IRA, you have "reduced" your income on which you have to pay taxes.

So, in this example, investing $2,000 in a traditional IRA actually only costs you $1,500 because you reduce your taxable income and the government reduces your income tax, essentially giving you free money.

A hint about getting more free money

Your family members may also recognize the importance of saving toward retirement. Discussing financial issues with your parents, aunts, uncles, and grandparents may impress them and encourage them to help. Try making a deal with them in order to help you establish your financial foundation. Again, in order for this to work, you need at least $250 in taxable income reported to the government.

Here's the premise:

We just looked at an example of reducing your taxable income to have the government give you free money. By investing in an IRA, you reduce your taxable income and save on the amount of money due in income taxes. Amazingly, the money that you invest in an IRA doesn't necessarily have to come from your earnings. The money can come from anywhere, assuming that you have the minimum annual income to qualify.

Here's the plan:

Tell your extended family that you want to open an IRA as an early start toward your financial dreams. Explain to them that you also understand that the investment to the IRA will reduce your income taxes. Instead of birthday gifts, ask them to give you money for your IRA contribution.

Here's how it works:

Your extended family will be so impressed with your knowledge of finances and your discipline in saving that, in many cases, they will agree to give you money for your IRA. In our experience, they will still give you birthday gifts, too! These IRA contributions can be made throughout the year, every year, so make sure you share with your family the progress you are making with your investments so they will continue to feel good about contributing to your cause.

Here's the bottom line:

Consider the first example in which you made $10,000 in a year and contributed $2,000 to your IRA, reducing your tax bill by $500. Now assume that you made $10,000 and you saved $2,000 but your family gave you $2,000 for your IRA. Take the money your family gave you and put it in your IRA. Again, your tax bill is reduced, but you still have your $2,000 in savings. You could contribute another $1,000 to your IRA that year, which would reduce your tax by an additional $250, or purchase mutual funds, stocks, or just save the money for your college fund, new car, or something else you may need.

More free money—Coverdell Education Savings Account

If you are under the age of eighteen, you automatically qualify for the Coverdell Education Savings Account. Formerly called the Education IRA, this is a method that enables you to save for qualified higher education expenses, including tuition, fees, books, supplies, and equipment. In fact, this money can be used to purchase a computer, software, and Internet access if it is needed for college, vocational, or public and private elementary, junior high and high schools.

When you are under the age of eighteen and open a Coverdell Education Savings Account, you can receive up to $2,000 per year in after-tax contributions from friends and relatives. Earnings in the account grow tax-free until distribution. Once you take money from the account, any money that has been in the account for five years can be withdrawn tax-free. Tax penalties may apply for withdrawals prior to five years from the time they were deposited. For example, if you deposited money into an account in 2006, you could withdraw the money in 2011 without penalty or taxes. However, if you deposited money in 2006 and withdrew it in 2007 or anytime before five years has passed, penalties would apply. The caveat is that all withdrawals must be made for qualified educational expenses.

Inform your parents and relatives that you are interested in opening a Coverdell Education Savings Account. Explain to them that you are interested in saving for college and that their contributions will help you achieve your educational goals. Chances are that your parents will be excited about your efforts to help fund the cost of college and may contribute to the plan on your behalf.

401(k) Accounts

In 1978, section 401(k) of the Internal Revenue Code authorized the use of a new type of defined contribution plan for employees to make pre-tax contributions to retirement savings. The retirement plans are called 401(k) plans, and are provided by most corporations. There are other versions of similar plans, known as a 403(b) or 457(g), but the 401(k) is the terminology we'll use.

Employees participating in a 401(k) plan through their employer make automatic payroll deductions before tax is calculated. This is known as *pretax contribution*. The contributions are invested at the employee's discretion into one or more funds provided in the plan. To encourage employees to invest, some employers choose to "match" employee contributions by adding a certain amount of money to an employee's 401(k) based on what the employee contributes. While the investments grow in the 401(k) account, the employees do not pay any taxes on them.

401k plans are good investment options, and the following describes some of the incentives for participating.

- **Company Match:**

  As an incentive to participate in the plan, many companies offer *matching*, in which the company will contribute a certain amount to your account for every dollar that you contribute, up to a certain limit. Think of matching as free money. You should be investing anyway, so take advantage of this opportunity by investing the maximum amount required to qualify for company matching.

- **Save while you increase your take-home pay:**

  This concept only makes sense when you consider the tax-deferred savings benefit of a 401(k) plan. Tax-deferred means that you pay no tax on the contribution or the growth of the investment until you withdraw it from the plan. When you invest pre-tax money, you are also decreasing your taxable income.

The following chart shows an example of how contributing to a 401(k) plan compares with saving outside the plan in a taxable account:

	With 401(k)	Without 401(k)
Annual Gross Salary	$50,000	$50,000
6% of pay before tax	-$3,000	$0
Taxable Income	$47,000	$50,000
27% Federal Income Tax	-$12,690	-$13,500
6% of pay after tax (for taxable savings)	$0	-$3,000
Take Home Pay	$34,310	$33,500
Difference in Take Home Pay	**$810**	

According to the chart, investing $3,000 in a 401(k) versus in a taxable account will provide you with considerable cash flow because the amount invested directly reduces your tax liability.

- **Professional Management:**

Many of the investment options in a 401(k) plan are mutual funds, which are largely managed by investment professionals (see Mutual Fund section). Therefore, the money you invest in mutual funds within your 401(k) plan can be managed by professionals so that you don't have to.

- **Liquidity:**

Although 401(k) plans are designed for retirement savings, many plans allow you to receive money from the plan if you need it. This can either be through loans or withdrawals. When you take a loan from your 401(k), you are essentially borrowing from yourself. To pay the loan back, you make payments with interest back to your account. Withdrawals are not as simple or advantageous. An early withdrawal from your plan should be made as a last resort because an unqualified withdrawal will result in the tax liability you've been avoiding by contributing to a tax-deferred account. In other words, if you don't follow the rules, the government will want their tax money, plus penalties.

- **Automatic Payroll Deduction:**

Contributing to your 401(k) is simple because the money is taken directly from your pay before you receive your paycheck. This is one of the most disciplined investment strategies because you can't spend what you don't have. Automatic payroll deductions equate to automatic investing using *dollar-cost averaging*, which is a great investment strategy. Dollar-cost averaging means that you invest the same amount every period, buying more units when prices are low and fewer units when prices are high.

- **Portability:**

In most cases, when you change jobs you can take your 401(k) with you. You may rollover your plan into a new company-sponsored 401(k) or you may keep your old account and start a new one with your new employer. Likewise, you can roll your old 401(k) account into an individual retirement account (IRA) and start a new 401(k) plan with your new employer. The bottom line: 401(k) accounts are generally portable.

- **Contribution Limits**

Although a 401(k) or 403(b) plan is one of the best investment options available, there are limits to the amount you can contribute annually. Through 2008, the annual limit for all Americans was $15,000 per year. Because these plans are relatively new, the government decided to allow "catch-up" contributions for people nearing retirement, and have gradually increased their contribution limits. Catch-up contributions are only for workers who are at least fifty years of age, so will not be discussed in this book.

Ready, Set, Invest

By now you should have a checking or savings account to keep your money. If you have taxable income during this year, or expect taxable income in later years, first consider opening an IRA with your savings in order to reduce your taxes, which we previously described.

Once you have funded your IRA, or if you don't want to lock away your money until you are sixty years old, consider investing in mutual funds and stocks. Notice that we said mutual funds *before* stocks. We did that on purpose. Investing in mutual funds is much easier and less risky than investing in individual stocks. Get your feet wet by investing in mutual funds, and then consider individual stocks.

There are two main ways to invest in mutual funds and stocks: through a broker or directly through the mutual fund company. We previously discussed opening a brokerage account and the different types of brokerages that are available. In most cases, unless you want to invest in individual stocks, a brokerage account is not necessary. Mutual funds can be purchased from mutual fund companies, but you need to understand your mutual fund strategy. If you want to invest in individual stocks, we will talk a bit about selecting individual stocks to purchase, although we want to reinforce that it can be very difficult to achieve long-term growth with individual stocks, especially if you don't have large sums of money to reduce your risk by diversifying across multiple stock types.

Finding the right mutual funds

When it comes to finding mutual funds, your options are numerous. As we discussed in the section on mutual funds, there are many different classes of funds and each has its own investment philosophy.

A popular way to begin investing in mutual funds is to open an account with a large *no-load mutual fund* company, such as Vanguard. A no-load mutual fund does not charge an up-front fee for investing in the fund. Vanguard, as well as many other mutual fund companies, has many different funds to choose from in a variety of investment classes. Additionally, when you have an account at one of these firms, it is easy to transfer money between different funds if your goals change. Also, when your money isn't invested in a fund, it is normally placed in a money market mutual fund, which is similar to a savings account but usually with higher interest rates. You can also buy funds through your brokerage account; however, some mutual funds provide lower minimum investments when you open an account directly with the mutual fund company.

Mutual funds are the easiest and safest way to invest in the stock market. Odds are that you are not a stock market expert who can spend all day analyzing which stocks to hold in your account. Most people are not stock market experts, which explains the popularity of mutual funds. Mutual funds are managed by people who get paid based upon how well a fund performs. Leave the stock selecting to the experts and find the mutual fund that is right for you.

Consider the Index Fund

An even simpler method of picking mutual funds is to stick with the funds that track the major indexes. These are funds that track the Dow, NASDAQ, and S&P 500. Because index-tracking funds require less research than other specific mutual funds, their costs are generally lower. If your goal is long-term growth of your money without worrying about fund philosophy (who, where, and why in which the fund invests), index funds are a great choice.

An index fund buys all the stocks in a chosen index to represent that market segment. The S&P index is primarily composed of large stocks, while the NASDAQ Composite index is heavy with technology companies. When you buy an index fund, you are trying to match the performance of the group of stocks that comprise the index. For example, when the news reports the DJIA changed one percent for a particular day, the DJIA Index Fund should have changed by one percent as well.

Consider the Vanguard 500 Index fund. This has become one of the largest mutual funds in the world, mostly because it has had a history of good performance. In fact, over the past ten years, the Vanguard 500 Index fund has outperformed almost all of the other funds that are out there today[4].

More information on the Vanguard 500 Index fund can be found at: Vanguard, *www.vanguard.com,* (800) 662-7447.

The drawback to investing directly with mutual fund companies such as Vanguard is that you can only invest in the funds that the company manages. If you find funds from several different fund companies that you want to invest in, it might be a better idea to invest in them through a brokerage account. This will require some analysis on your part, especially with regard to the fees associated with owning multiple funds through a brokerage. After all, the broker is a middleman between you and the mutual fund companies; they charge for that service. In most cases, the cheapest and easiest way to begin investing in mutual funds is directly through the mutual fund company.

Investing in stocks

Stock investing can be very simple or very complex. Stock investing strategies, such as types of orders, margin trading, options, and hedging are beyond the scope of this book and will not be covered. Many books exist on each of those topics and we encourage you to continue your financial education by learning about them when you feel comfortable with the basic information we have presented.

---

4   http://www.vanguard.com

Considerations for picking stocks

Before we discuss different ways to pick individual stocks, let's first ask a few questions about your daily routine:

1. If you wake up in the morning and turn on the TV, which morning program do you watch?

2. In the shower, which products do you always use?

3. Do you normally eat the same breakfast?

4. What kind of car do you drive to school?

5. Where do you most like to eat lunch?

6. Where do you like to go out for dinner?

Are you wondering why we're asking such questions? The answers to these questions can become the basis of your stock investing ideas. If you wake up in the morning with *The Today Show* (part of General Electric, NYSE: GE), shower with Dial soap (NYSE: DL), eat Cheerios or Wheaties for breakfast (General Mills, NYSE: GIS), drive a Chevrolet to school (part of General Motors, NYSE: GM), eat lunch at McDonalds (NYSE: MCD) and eat out at Chili's or Macaroni Grill for dinner (part of Brinker Corporation, NYSE: EAT), these all might be good ideas for individual stock investments. Peter Lynch, an author and former manager of Fidelity's Magellan mutual fund, has written for years about the benefit of ordinary investors taking note of which products and companies they like, and using that as a starting point for investment ideas[5].

Why should you invest in a small telecom equipment company when you could invest in the company that provides your food, gas, or other needs? Wouldn't you be more inclined to recognize patterns in the companies you frequent than those you know little about? This is the most important activity in individual stock investing—paying attention to the company issuing the underlying stock.

---

5   http://www.fidelity.com

Once you identify some companies that you might be interested in investing with, you want to do some homework on the company's financial health. Is the company growing? Does the company carry a high level of debt? Is the company's stock under-priced compared to its industry peers? These and many other factors should be considered before investing in stocks. Many books, brokerage and investing web sites, financial planners, and brokers are good resources that can teach you more about buying and selling stocks.

Regardless of whether you purchased mutual funds or individual stocks, either through an IRA account or a brokerage, keep in mind that your goal is long-term growth of your money. Don't labor over the stock and mutual fund pages every day to see what your investments are doing. We mentioned that, over the long term, the overall value of the stock market has grown, but there have been several short periods in history in which stock prices have dropped significantly. If you see that your stock or mutual fund is losing money, don't panic and sell it unless you have a good reason, such as corporate scandals or financial problems that could bankrupt the company in which you are invested. With long-term investment goals in mind, you should be able to weather short-term declines and benefit from long-term growth.

Long-term investing is a slow process, but the sooner you get started, the more time your money has to grow. Try to systematically invest a certain amount of money every month or every year in any or all of the methods we have discussed. Investing is not difficult. Get started, have fun, and watch your money grow.

Taxes

If you have ever overheard your parents discussing taxes, chances are that they didn't have many good things to say. Nearly everyone dislikes paying taxes, but not only is paying taxes required by law, it is also an obligation of every wage-earning U.S. citizen. More often than not, people complain about taxes but still expect the police to keep them safe, the firefighters to come in case of a fire, and the roads and highways to be in good shape. All of these services and many more are paid with tax dollars. In fact, most of the social services that protect us (and that we generally take for granted) are primarily funded through tax dollars. So as painful as paying taxes might be, you should know that by paying them you are a contributing member of society.

We previously discussed the tax withholdings from your paycheck, so you probably understand how you pay taxes every pay period. The exercise that most people loathe is filing taxes. Federal taxes for a given calendar year must be filed by April 15th the following year.

Sometime in January or February, you will receive a tax booklet from the government with information about filing your taxes for the previous calendar year. You will also receive a statement from your employer (a W-2) with the information needed to complete your tax forms.

The federal tax laws are extremely complicated and can take volumes to explain. We won't go into too much detail regarding tax laws because most of them won't apply to you anyway. Luckily for us, the government recognizes that millions of taxpayers don't need all the complicated forms and only require one easy-to-complete document: the 1040-EZ.

A vast majority of teenagers can file taxes using the 1040-EZ form. The most common requirements are as follows: you must earn less than $50,000 per year and you cannot itemize deductions. An appendix to this book contains a section on completing the 1040-EZ form, which you can refer to at the appropriate time.

If you only have income from a part-time job and you are not claiming that you are "exempt" from paying taxes, chances are that you will receive a tax refund. As nice as it is to get a check back from the government, keep in mind that any overpayment to the government is, effectively, an interest-free loan you are making. Don't maximize your tax withholdings just to receive a large tax refund the following year. You can do better things with your money than loan it to the government. Also, if you are due a refund, beware of the services that provide you with a "tax refund advance" or a "tax refund anticipation" loan. These services are similar to payday loans, and are not a good deal.

Conclusion:
A Checklist

Well done for taking charge of your financial future! If you made it this far, you have taken a big step toward your financial independence. As you have probably realized, the process toward financial freedom does not happen overnight—it takes hard work, determination, a consistent approach, and, most of all, time.

The following checklist is for future reference as you progress down your own path to financial independence. Check off items that you have completed and identify what other items need to be addressed to meet your goals. Although you may mark "Setting Goals" as completed, make sure you revisit your goals, as well as the checklist below, to make sure you are making the necessary changes in your financial strategy in order to meet your new objectives.

- **Set your goals.** Write down your one-year, three-year, five-year, and ten-year goals.

- **Set a budget and stick to it.** Track how much you are spending versus how much you are earning. It will help you keep your spending under control and result in you keeping more of your hard-earned money.

- **Always think about the differences between needs and wants.** If you understand the differences in your day-to-day purchases, it is easier to earmark money for saving and investing rather than spending.

- **Open a bank account.** Open checking and savings accounts after shopping around for the best rates and lowest fees.

- **Understand your paycheck.** Not only will understanding your paycheck alert you to potential errors your employer may make, it will also help you realize the value of a dollar earned after paying your obligatory taxes.

- **Pay yourself first.** From each and every paycheck, put as much as you can afford into your savings or investment accounts before paying any bills. Your savings is more important than your cell phone, so pay yourself first and *don't touch that savings.*

- **Balance your bank accounts.** Banks make mistakes. You won't know about them if you don't balance your bank accounts. Balancing your account will also provide you with the information you need to see if your current financial behavior is leading you toward or away from your financial goals.

- **Be cautious about using other people's money.** Every time you spend money that doesn't belong to you, you risk your financial independence. Banks charge more for lending you money than they pay to keep your money, and credit card companies are infamous for leading irresponsible consumers into financial jeopardy.

- **Read the fine print.** This includes the literature credit card companies send out as well as the loan documents you sign for a car loan, personal loan, or student loan. What you don't know *will* hurt you.

- **To invest in stocks, open a brokerage account.** You can open a full-service, discount, or online account to buy and sell stocks.

- **To invest in mutual funds, try the direct route.** Although a brokerage can buy and sell mutual funds for you, you can do it cheaper by going directly to the source of the mutual fund, such as Vanguard or Fidelity Investments.

- **File your income taxes.** You have probably heard the saying that "the only guarantees in life are death and taxes." Avoid the strong arm of the IRS by filing your taxes accurately and on time.

- **Don't be a victim of identity theft.** Identity theft is a rapidly growing problem that can significantly set back your financial progress. Understand how to protect yourself and take preventative measures regularly. Protect your personal information such as your social security number, passwords, and account numbers. Use a shredder to destroy documents containing your personal and financial information.

And now the most important item of all....

- **GET STARTED NOW!** Time is on your side, but the longer you wait, the less the power of time will work for you. Whatever you can scrape together to invest today has the potential to pay dividends in the future, leading you to financial freedom sooner. Go talk to your parents, your grandparents, your teacher, or your friends to let them know that you are starting your journey to financial independence and you want them support you with their ideas.

- If you need help along the way, please contact us at http://www.theteensguide.com

Appendix:
Completing the 1040-EZ Tax Form

Although the name of the tax document implies that it is "easy" to complete, this term is only relative to the difficulty of the "1040-not-EZ." Since tax forms can be confusing, we are here to help.

First, make sure you have all of the necessary documentation, which could include your W-2 (summary of earnings from your employer), 1099 forms (summary of interest, dividends and stock or mutual fund sales from your bank/brokerage accounts) and evidence of your IRA contribution, if applicable. Because we are discussing the 1040-EZ form, we are assuming that you aren't itemizing deductions and are just taking the standard tax deduction.

The first section of the 1040-EZ is very simple—just enter your name, address and social security number. Make sure you double and triple-check that your social security number is correct. If you enter the wrong social security number, your refund may be sent to someone else, and the IRS might come after you, thinking that you never filed your return. Again, make sure your social security number is accurate.

The next line asks if you want to contribute $3 to the presidential election campaign. Federal elections are primarily funded through federal money, which includes the amount of funds taxpayers agree to contribute on their tax returns. Whether you check "Yes" or "No" on this section will not impact your tax liability.

The next section of the 1040-EZ is called "Income" and looks similar to the table below.

1 Wages, Salaries, and Tips	$
2 Taxable Interest	$
3 Unemployment compensation, etc.	$
4 Adj. Gross Income (Add lines 1, 2, and 3)	$
5 Can your parents claim you as dependent?	Amount will vary based on answer
6 Taxable Income (Subtract line 5 from line 4)	$

On line 1 of this section, enter the amount from box 1 of your W-2, called Wages, Salaries, and Tips. On line 2 of the form, enter the amount of interest you received from your bank or money market account. If you have multiple accounts, you must add all of the interest together and put the sum on the tax form. Unless you receive unemployment benefits or other special circumstances apply, you can leave line 3 blank. On line 4, add lines 1 through 3 in the income section. Line 5 of this section is where the form can get a little tricky. In most cases, teenagers are still listed as dependents on their parent's tax returns. Therefore, you would check the "Yes" box stating that someone can claim you as a dependent. If you check this box, there is a worksheet on the back of the form to complete. The instructions for this worksheet are very simple, so we won't cover it here. Just fill out the forms as requested and make the necessary calculations with a calculator. Once you complete the worksheet, transfer the figure to line 5 of the 1040-EZ. On line 6, you subtract your deduction from line 5 from your total income on line 4. This number represents your taxable income.

The next section is called "Payments and Tax" and is similar to the table below.

7 Fed. Income Tax Withheld	$
8 Earned Income Credit	$
9 Total Payments (add lines 7 and 8)	$
10 Tax (from tax tables)	$
11 Refund (if line 9 is larger than line 10, subtract line 10 from line 9)	$
12 Tax Due (if line 10 is larger than line 9, subtract line 9 from line 10)	$

On line 7, enter the number listed in box 2 of your W-2 called "Federal income tax withheld." This is the amount of money the government took from all of your paychecks during the year. Line 8 of this section is rare for teenagers, so we won't cover it here. Line 9 is the sum of lines 7 and 8 and is the total amount of taxes you paid during the year. On line 10, you must refer to the instruction booklet that comes with the 1040-EZ form to determine how much tax you are required to pay. The table is very easy to follow, and just transfer the appropriate number to line 10.

If line 9 (total taxes paid) is greater than line 10 (total tax due), subtract line 10 from line 9 and put the number in line 11. This is your tax refund. If the opposite is true (line 10 is greater than line 9), subtract line 9 from line 10 and enter the number in line 12. This is the amount of tax you owe.

Finally, make sure you sign and date the tax form. Millions of people every year spend hours and hours on their tax forms, but then forget to sign them. The IRS will reject your form if it is not signed. Also, make sure you put your tax form, along with any requested documentation such as W-2's, and payment (if you owe additional taxes) in the mail on or before April 15th. Your tax return must be postmarked by this date or you could face penalties for late filing.

978-0-595-50969-0
0-595-50969-X

LaVergne, TN USA
22 January 2010
170806LV00004B/51/P